Bernard Bosanquet

The Civilization of Christendom

And Other Studies

Bernard Bosanquet

The Civilization of Christendom
And Other Studies

ISBN/EAN: 9783337022587

Printed in Europe, USA, Canada, Australia, Japan

Cover: Foto ©Lupo / pixelio.de

More available books at **www.hansebooks.com**

The Ethical Library

THE CIVILIZATION OF CHRISTENDOM

AND OTHER STUDIES

BY

BERNARD BOSANQUET,

M.A. (Oxon.), Hon. LL.D. (Glasgow)
Formerly Fellow of University College, Oxford

London
SWAN SONNENSCHEIN & CO.
NEW YORK: MACMILLAN & CO.
1893

Butler & Tanner,
The Selwood Printing Works,
Frome, and London.

PREFACE.

THE following Addresses are printed so far as possible in the form in which they were delivered. But in some cases they were not fully written out before delivery, and have unavoidably been modified in preparation for the press. My thanks are due to the proprietors of the *International Journal of Ethics* and of the *Charity Organisation Review* for permission to reprint two of them. The various Societies before which the addresses were given, including the London Ethical Society, are of course not responsible for the views expressed in them.

In the paper on Individualism and Socialism there is one point which I desire to modify. I think that I was wrong in favouring a differential Poor Law treatment of persons who have shown signs of thrift. Classification within Poor Law institutions, which is certainly desirable, should, I now think, be guided by present differences of age, sex, behaviour, physical condition, and sensitiveness. But differential treatment on account of past conduct seems to me a principle not reconcilable with the proper working of the Poor Law, and tending to widen the area of dependence on it. Outside the Poor Law, by pensions and analogous methods, such treatment may very well be provided through the neighbourly kindness of individuals.

On another point, that of thrift or saving as a working-class policy, I see signs of approximation between the two most antagonistic opinions. We, the advocates of thrift, have always insisted on the value of " constructive " saving,—saving embodied in the health and well-being of the family, and in the niceness of the home. Our opponents, I think, are beginning to recognise the value of organised insurance, *e.g.* against the breadwinner's illness, from which the physical and moral ruin of the family, if unprepared, so constantly takes its rise. The still fundamental difference between us springs in a great measure from differing experience. We mean by " thrift " and " unthriftiness " what we see from day to day in the British working-class. Thrift is, for us, the germ of the capacity to look at life as a whole, and organise it. It involves a recognition both of the area of life, as including the family and others whose security from disaster depends on the individual's prudence, and also of its duration, as a lapse of time for which, and not merely for a few days or weeks, he must lay his account. Life thus looked at implies a higher, not a lower standard of comfort, a more generous and not a more grudging acceptance of obligation, than the life of those who have never learnt to look beyond the passing day and their most single self, and in whose household there is no more care for the family than there is for the future. The latter are the unthrifty, as we practically know them. They do not *spend* in the sense which our opponents approve ; they waste and muddle away their resources. There are other senses in which the terms "thrifty" and "unthrifty" may be used, and upon them our judgment might be different. But it is plain that thrift, as above described, that is thrift as we employ the term (and this is the meaning which applies in English life), is the polar opposite of an "individualistic" quality. And yet, making life as a whole the standard of comfort, it does not abate, but rather increases, the worker's just demands.

The careless current usage of such terms as "individualistic," "socialistic," "egoistic," "altruistic," is a discredit to the popular theory of an age which professes to be critical. If some of our very able writers of Ethical manuals would give all these expressions a thorough shaking-out before the public, they would do a good deed. Meantime, I hope that these Addresses may be of use or interest to some besides those who have already heard them.

BERNARD BOSANQUET.

August, 1893.

CONTENTS.

CHAPTER		PAGE
I.	FUTURE OF RELIGIOUS OBSERVANCE	1
II.	SOME THOUGHTS ON THE TRANSITION FROM PAGANISM TO CHRISTIANITY	27
III.	THE CIVILIZATION OF CHRISTENDOM	63
IV.	OLD PROBLEMS UNDER NEW NAMES	100
V.	ARE WE AGNOSTICS?	127
VI.	THE COMMUNICATION OF MORAL IDEAS AS A FUNCTION OF AN ETHICAL SOCIETY	160
VII.	RIGHT AND WRONG IN FEELING	208
VIII.	TRAINING IN ENJOYMENT	237
IX.	LUXURY AND REFINEMENT	268
X.	THE ANTITHESIS BETWEEN INDIVIDUALISM AND SOCIALISM PHILOSOPHICALLY CONSIDERED	304
XI.	LIBERTY AND LEGISLATION	358

I.

THE FUTURE OF RELIGIOUS OBSERVANCE.[1]

I HAVE no dogma to put before you upon this very difficult question. I propose that we should simply direct our attention to it. It is well sometimes to let our thoughts play freely upon such a subject, to walk round the mountain and look at it with a glass, instead of trying to ascend it. Suitably to such a purpose, I will begin from the outside of the problem, by considering how certain kinds of change would strike us in an English village or town.

The question is whether we think that any

---

[1] Delivered before the Progressive Society.

form of distinctively religious observance will long survive our present orthodox Sabbatarianism. I mean by "religious," for our present purpose, something generally and obviously taken as symbolic of the best we know; something allied to public worship and public observance of the Sunday; not anything that presupposes special training or special knowledge or specially acquired interest.

We may assume that we shall have art, literature and science, and also associated efforts of many kinds, which will bring people together in the sympathy of a common cause and a common pursuit of good. But all this will be special, and people will sort themselves in regard to it according to their tastes and capacities. Will there, we further ask, be religious observance, ceremonial, meeting, or general abstinence from work on Sunday with any significance beyond that of a Bank Holiday, over and above our private and specialised endeavours towards the best life ?

At present the dominant Sabbatarianism answers these questions even for us who have no belief in its grounds. It protects us and impresses us more than we know. On Sunday we have either a social and domestic day, or a quiet day. If we go out to lecture or to be lectured to, we are within the great analogy of Sunday observance. I never pass along the main thoroughfare of my district on a Sunday evening, having some such errand in view, without being reminded, by the sight of the street preachers, how all-pervading is the sentiment which sends us out on that particular day. Where ethical meetings are held on a week-day, their nature has appeared to me to be somewhat different. They then take the form rather of special discussions than of general appeals. Owing to the pervading sentiment which survives, the question what is permissible on a Sunday is not yet raised in extreme forms. We rail at Sabbatarianism, but we have hardly thought how we should get on without any Sunday at all.

Now what is likely to happen,—what do we want to happen, — assuming that we have merely to consider the permanent needs and tendencies of ordinary people, without reference to any authority beyond these needs themselves? Is it likely that Sunday will continue to differ at all from a week-day, on which we happen not to be at work?

To what use, for example, will the fabrics of the churches be turned? If there is Sunday worship, that will go far to settle the whole matter of Sunday observance. Therefore the existence of these fabrics, though in one sense a mere external circumstance, is yet a very important point.

Let us think of a country village, with a fine old church before the very doors of the houses, in which there is a good organ and a fair musical service is held, forming the centre of a certain amount of musical training among the people. There may seldom be any sense talked in the pulpit, but yet the place is a sort of social focus. The crises of life receive through it, as it were, a social sanction—infancy, maturity, marriage and death are officially brought to public cognisance and sympathy.

Now, suppose—as the simplest expression of complete national neutrality—that the Church were disestablished on the old Radical lines. The fabric would then belong, I imagine, to an exasperated sect, whose members would have to maintain it. For a long time its old prestige would continue, and wealthy persons would be found to meet the cost of maintenance. But one day the actual situation would exert its influence; many would abandon the sect in possession, which would become narrower and still more exasperated, and an apple of discord would have been planted in the centre of the village, many of whose inhabitants would feel themselves ousted from the old church at their doors. One would hope that some village hall or music-room would assert itself as a centre, where all might unite on occasions of general interest, and that the schism would not be intensified by the establishment of a chapel beside the old church. Such a schism would no doubt prolong a definite observance of Sunday, and definite forms of worship—for competition is the soul of business—but it would do so under the most unhealthy conditions. It would be better that all the antagonism should be on one side, and that the village hall should become the centre of lectures or music or public ceremonies, and

Sunday observance should continue or not simply on its merits, as the needs of the people might dictate.

If, again, as has been suggested in recent years, the fabric of the church were left to the ratepayers, the question would arise whether they would care to support it. If not, the old building would become a ruin, or would be kept in order by the public spirit of some individual. The general course of public observance in the village would be the same as in the former case, only without the schism, unless, indeed, the disestablished sect should purchase the building from the ratepayers. If the old building became a ruin, or show place, and the life of the village centred round a lecture hall or music-room, that would be a clean cut between old and new, and in some ways a healthy thing. The church building would be no great practical loss, for it is seldom really well fitted either for speaking or for music ; and the moral emancipation of the little community would be visibly symbolised. On the other hand, it would be somewhat strange and sad to have an old ruin, or an unused building kept up from merely antiquarian interest, in the centre of half the villages in England.

But if the ratepayers chose to maintain and use the building, in a way more or less continuous with that previously practised, it might perhaps become a valuable centre of their social life and religious observance. The public element which the Church now represents, both in its cognisance of incidents concerning the individual and the nation, and, perhaps, through the Christmas festival and the harvest home, would be the typical nucleus of its functions. There might be weekly musical services, and addresses from persons chosen by the community, on the duties of citizenship, or on the significance of great movements and personalities in history, or at the present day. The possibilities of village life have not yet been thoroughly studied; but there are phenomena which point to a development that will expel the countryman of comic tradition from the ideas of our age.

In this alternative we should have realised what has been called " the disestablishment of the clergy, and not of the Church."

Whether all this is or is not chimerical, I am strongly of opinion that the existence of our country churches, with their beauty and their central position and traditional importance in our villages, cannot be disregarded in considering the future of Sunday observance. Even those who care least about them now would be annoyed to see others in possession of them, and to be excluded from them in those incidents of life to which they communicate a well-recognised dignity. And if the Athenian made his oath of service to the community on becoming of age to bear arms, I do not see why we should not have a rational confirmation ceremony, at which the individual should accept for himself the vows and intentions which, whether in church or out of church, his parents have surely conceived on his behalf.

The question of buildings is, in one sense, still more pressing in such cities as have ancient churches or cathedrals of national value. We can neither give up our minsters and our abbeys to a sect, nor permit them to fall into ruins. Are they then to be museums, like San Marco at Florence, where the *gendarme* watches the passing tourist in Savonarola's cell? It seems more probable that the fine services and the addresses of great preachers for which, say, Westminster Abbey has become famous, will gradually lose their dogmatic element, and widen into something that every one may value, while the funerals of famous men and other national acts may take place there, emphasised, perhaps, by speakers publicly appointed like Pericles at Athens.

Here we have, in an intensified form, the problem which we recognised in the case of the country churches. These great buildings will always favour a tendency to some kind, however simple, of general religious observance.

In the ordinary life of our great towns the matter is somewhat different. The dweller in a city has no relation to his local church. Its organisation is practically congregational, rather than territorial. An increasing proportion of the church buildings are hideous, and no one could desire to preserve them for their own sake. Of the people who care for religious observance, a very large fraction are Nonconformists. This brings us nearer to the inside of our question. Here we have to do with bodies of strongly convinced worshippers of all creeds, practically working on a congregational system, *i.e.* depending for the repute and splendour of their church upon the position it can make for itself. These people are set upon religious observance ; it seems a vital need to them, altogether apart from establishment, and from such local influences as operate in a country village. It is a striking sight to see a roomful of hard-headed mechanics in a factory town, listening to an address on Pauline theology, in the "adult Sunday-school" of a Nonconformist chapel.

Do we think, and do we wish, that Sunday should become like a Bank Holiday—a common non-working day—for the descendants of men like these ? Will something analogous to our own Ethical lectures serve as a meeting point for them, and as a means of guiding and concentrating their " cosmic emotion " ? May the Ethical teacher look for this ? There are many difficulties on both sides. There is the question of the young. Certainly one would wish that they should be helped and guided towards the higher side of feeling and reflection. But yet it is, perhaps, a pitfall to try and keep up religious observances only for the young. It tends to a division in life, and probably to hypocrisy on the part of the elders ; to a different version of the view that "Religion, though a virtue in the female, is undoubtedly a defect in the male." Good schools and healthy home life will do a great deal for the young, without specific religious teaching.

I will suggest my own ideas merely as an illustration.

First as to Sunday in general. I assume that it remains the practically universal holiday. If not,—if, for example, different trades take their holidays on different days of the week, that destroys Sunday so far as the law is concerned ; there would then be no question of closing shops and stopping factories on one day more than another. But, taking it as the universal holiday, I may be old-fashioned, but I do not think that I want the present law to be altered. It alone protects Sunday from the whole set of amusements which are carried on for profit—horseracing, cricket, football, and athletics with gate money, the music halls and theatres. Of course, if the law could distinguish, one would like good concerts and, perhaps, some theatres to be open. But the law cannot, I presume, distinguish between performances carried on for profit. I see no way out of it but to maintain the prohibition of entertainments for profit, while throwing open without payment all public places of higher recreation, and providing music in the parks. Associations might well be formed to give musical performances, as at the People's Palace, in public halls, especially during the winter. The prohibition of profit furnishes a fair negative test of quality. As a rule people would not trouble themselves to give performances free, unless they really believed that what they gave was worth giving in the general interest.

Thus I should hope that before our Sabbatarianism is destroyed we may have utilised it to found a new kind of Sunday—an English Sunday, not a Puritan nor yet a Parisian Sunday. We have a great and grave responsibility in this matter. We are working to destroy superstition.   Are we or are we not aiming at such a result that the Derby will be run on Sunday, or the " Gentlemen and Players " played, or the Oxford and Cambridge boat-race rowed on Sunday ?   Well, I hope not.   I should like to see grow up a tradition of family reunion (which is impossible for the working class on a day when many kinds of labour go on), of the simpler kinds of social reunion, of healthy country recreation, of occupation with art, music, and literature, and with the beauties of Nature.   Games, of course, would be the rule for private amusement, but I should hope that the huge machinery of Lord's and the Oval would not be set in motion.   If, however, one were forced to choose, I believe the Bank Holiday Sunday would be better than the Puritan Sunday.

Secondly, as to more strictly ceremonial observance.   Out of what needs does it spring ?

I have tried to explain that I have some belief in the social recognition of great moments both in national and individual life. I incline to think that, whether in a public hall or in a church, some little solemnity at the critical points of life, with a few words spoken by a man or woman of intelligence and position, might be of service. But again, no doubt, it might be ridiculous, according to the turn taken by the national mind.

As to the continuance of any regular system of meeting together week by week, among whole sets of neighbours, to participate in music or congregational singing, or to listen to lectures or addresses, we have several points to consider. Lectures of this kind descend from the sermon; and the sermon, I presume, from an age when the preacher was more educated than his hearers; and certainly from a time when he is supposed to have some

key, which they had not, to religious knowledge.

Conditions of this kind are quickly disap-
pearing now, and in the time to which we look
forward no trace of them will remain. *Now* it
is a great thing merely to meet a few sympathis-
ing friends. *Then* we may hope that in the
main all society will be sympathetic in a more
rational standpoint. *Now* we are just breaking
through to free thought, and we are struggling
with great ideas as to the way of regarding
life and duty and what is best in the world.
But *then* we shall no longer have the strenuous
virtues of the minority, but our danger will lie
in the inertia of our majority. Our general
standpoint will have lost the excitement of
novelty, and we shall be forming a new
orthodoxy. *Now* there is only beginning to be
a widespread system of first-rate University
teaching made accessible throughout the

country, and the Ethical lecturer, if he is about as well qualified as an Extension lecturer, may break new ground and reach new audiences. But *then*, I sincerely hope, the Sunday lecturer will be, at best, but one among a number of teachers, from whom any student will be able to learn under conditions no less stimulating than on Sunday, and more solidly and systematically. A teacher who tries to deal with life in general is indeed almost certain, in an age of universal education, to be behind a great part of his audience in every distinct matter he may touch upon; and if this false direction, as I think it, is adopted, the lecturer of the future will have as little that can interest his audience as the preacher of to-day.

It appears, therefore, very doubtful whether instruction or oratory can ever take the place of public worship. Instruction essentially deals with special matter, while public worship is supposed to meet a general need ; and with the abandonment of public worship as a service of prayer and praise to a common Father, it appears to me that the only general source of cosmic emotion has ceased to exist, and that the world will have to rely on more concrete forms of sympathy depending on more definite common experience and common interest.   A congregation gathered together owing to mere local proximity would hardly—if I am right— have enough in common to supply matter to a teacher or preacher week after week through- out the year.   We see the strain and perversion and artificiality, induced by the task of finding something to say about things in general for years together, even in the clergy to-day, who have at least to communicate a definite doctrine with a general bearing on life.   How much worse the risk of platitude and rhetoric will be when the preacher has nothing to tell except what every sensible man knows as well as he! Therefore, I should have hoped that Sunday would come to be marked, as it now is in many happy households, rather by a peculiar tone which attaches to its occupations than by any distinct habit of meeting or of ritual. The rule on which this tone might be founded would be suggested by the public authority, if it adopted the attitude which I have advocated, viz. that the day should indeed be a general holiday, but one on which, *comparatively speaking*, families and individuals should be thrown on their own resources for entertainment. I should hope that circles of friends, and families, would find out, as so many already do, higher interests to pursue, more appropriate, more profound, more continuous, and more ardent, than is possible for a general congregation brought together at random.

It may seem that these suggestions herald a

splitting up of culture which will destroy unity and sympathy. I do not think so. The open secret of modern life, to my mind, is that we find the universal not in the general, but in the individual. If our interest, for example, is in fine art, we need not keep drawing back and dallying with ethics or history for fear we should become one-sided. We should go right in as deep and thoroughly as we can, and we shall find our ethics and history, though in another form, when we have gone deep enough.

So I say that I hope a definite tradition will form itself, that it is a duty, especially on the weekly holiday, to renew our hold, first indeed, if necessary,—as it is for those who rarely meet, —on our families and friends, and then on those works of man and nature which best typify to us the unity of the world. It has been said that it is a duty to hear or read or see something very good every day. We who are less fortunately situated might compromise perhaps upon " every week." But we ought not to be governed simply by historical inheritance in the form which we give to this aspiration, and we ought always to aim, for ourselves and others, at an interest which is continuous and penetrating, so that our emotional life may be fed with realities, and we may lay hands on something which will not crumble in our grasp.

Especially I would suggest that the employment of simple music as an accompaniment to prayer and praise has nothing in common with the strictly æsthetic enjoyment and exaltation proper to the great musical art which we delight in for its own sake at a concert. It seems, therefore, altogether a mistake to introduce a concert into a service, or to turn a service into a concert. A good concert is a good Sunday occupation,—none better; but it is not appropriate to a mixed congregation, for many of whom it is a trial, while those who enjoy it most do not enjoy an oration following it.

The literature of religious emotion, again,—as, for example, the Hebrew prophets,—seems to be rather a stimulant than a food. It does not expand into a world, it does not lead us continuously forward, but rather subjects us to recurrent excitements of feeling. The study of religions, on the other hand, is of course an interesting study, but must be clearly distinguished from the employment of religious literature for purposes of public worship or the utterance of a common feeling.

It seems, then, quite possible, that in spite of a sound tradition as to the use of the weekly holiday—in part, perhaps, because of such a tradition—we may in course of generations cease to possess or to recognise any general

external symbol of our common human relation
to the reality of what is best.   And so superficial and so ambiguous have such symbols
proved themselves, that the loss may well be a
gain.   Only let us remember that the abandonment of a symbol may always have two meanings.   It may indicate that we have surrendered
the thing signified, or it may indicate that we
have grasped it in a truer form.

It is not easy to be sure whether we are
wholly free from the former risk.   There is a
French expression, signifying "the average
sensual man," which Matthew Arnold frequently refers to.   Many things in modern
life have an appearance as if we were finding
our level in this direction.   If it were so, the
world would not be worth living in; and such
tendencies we must see to it that we resist; for
they would make life a baser thing than it ever
has been before.

But if by abandoning the general external symbol we indicate, and truly indicate, that we at last have felt in our hands and recognised in our lives the thing signified, the actual spiritual world in all its various reality, then, surely, life will be nobler than it ever has been before.

II.

SOME THOUGHTS ON THE TRANSITION FROM PAGANISM TO CHRISTIANITY.[1]

In spite of Gibbon, we still on the whole accept the general idea of the Christian era which St. Paul and other writers of that age have impressed upon the modern mind. We have not thoroughly readjusted our historical notions to critical and natural ideas. Even so great a scholar as Matthew Arnold does what he can to perpetuate a mysterious conception of the new birth of the world at the time of Christ's coming. Hear him in "Obermann Once More" :—

---

[1] Delivered at Essex Hall for the London Ethical Society.

" Perceivest thou not the change of day ?
　　Ah ! carry back thy ken,
What, some two thousand years !　Survey
　　The world as it was then.

Like ours it looked in outward air,
　　Its head was clear and true,
Sumptuous its clothing, rich its fare,
　　No pause its action knew.

Stout was its arm, each thew and bone
　　Seemed puissant and alive,—
But ah ! its heart, its heart was stone,
　　And so it could not thrive !

On that hard Pagan world disgust
　　And secret loathing fell ;
Deep weariness and sated lust
　　Made human life a hell.

In his cool hall, with haggard eyes,
　　The Roman noble lay ;
He drove abroad, in furious guise,
　　Along the Appian way.

He made a feast, drank fierce and fast,
　　And crowned his brow with flowers,
No easier nor no quicker passed
　　The impracticable hours.

The brooding East with awe beheld
   Her impious younger world,
The Roman tempest swelled and swelled
   And on her head was hurled.

The East bowed low before the blast
   In patient, deep disdain ;
She let the legions thunder past
   And plunged in thought again.

So well she mused, a morning broke
   Across her spirit grey ;
A conquering new-born joy awoke
   And filled her life with day.

' Poor world,' she cried, ' so deep accurst,
   That runn'st from pole to pole,
Go seek a draught to slake thy thirst,
   Go seek it in thy soul ! '

She heard it, the victorious West
   In crown and sword arrayed !
She felt the void which mined her breast,
   She shivered and obeyed.

She veiled her eagles, snapped her sword,
   And laid her sceptre down ;
Her stately purple she abhorred,
   And her imperial crown.

> She broke her flutes, she stopped her sports,
>   Her artists could not please ;
> She tore her books, she shut her courts,
>   She fled her palaces.
>
> Lust of the eye and pride of life,
>   She left it all behind,
> And hurried, torn with inward strife,
>   The wilderness to find.
>
> Tears washed the trouble from her face,
>   She changed into a child !
> 'Mid weeds and wrecks she stood—a place
>   Of ruin—but she smiled ! "

This general idea of the bankruptcy of Paganism is drawn from St. Paul and other early Christian controversialists, and from Roman satirists. Is it possible for us at all to clear up our conceptions on this matter—on the question how far Pagan life had, in the age which we are considering, become devoid of good, and how far, under Christian influence, it was broken down and flung aside, and re-placed by convictions and impulses that were wholly new ? The issue is one of immense scope, and demanding for its adequate statement—its complete solution is not to be looked for—a very rare equipment, which I do not possess, of historical and literary learning. I only propose to offer one or two hints as to points of view which may be of value in helping us to take our bearings with regard to it. The unquestioned facts with which we are confronted are such as these :—The existence of very terrible immorality and brutality in the wealthy and civilised Roman Empire ; the lack of the greatest original genius of any kind, outside war and politics, for fully 300 years before Christ ; and the startling phenomenon that a new sect, originating among poor and unlettered Jews, did, after about three centuries, become the official religion of the Roman Empire, and nominally ousted the Pagan Polytheism by a Monotheism derived from the Hebrew religion, though not identical with the form of Monotheism professed by the Hebrews.

For a thousand years, moreover, this sect, now the victorious Catholic Church, was the strongest power in the civilised world, and whatever its true intellectual origin may have been, acknowledged but a trifling debt to the previous Pagan civilisation, its attitude towards which was for the most part professedly hostile. This, so far, would suggest to us that the previous civilisation had very little of value to bequeath, and as a fact its art and philosophy *in the old form* were for the time totally extinguished by the new movement. The works of classical sculpture and painting were to a great extent defaced or destroyed. The philosophical schools of Athens were closed by Justinian in 529. In the western or Latin world the great Greek poets and philosophers gradually ceased to be read, and the books containing their works to be preserved as things of value, till finally the Greek language itself ceased to be known even to professed scholars and philosophers.[1]   In the year 393 A.D., we may add, further to illustrate Matthew Arnold's verses, the famous Olympic sports had come to an end, after a reputed continuance of eleven centuries. Hopes and beliefs, supposed to be entirely new and true, with a new literature and a new music and hymnology, occupied men's minds. A fragment of such a new chant is supposed to be preserved in the words—" Awake, thou that sleepest, and arise from the dead, and Christ shall give thee light." We are even told, by a leading critic,[2]

---

[1] *Scotus Erigena* (9th century A.D.), a really great thinker, was the last scholar who knew Greek before the dawn of the Renaissance, and his knowledge was exceedingly imperfect.

[2] Prof. Harnack in *Encycl. Brit.*, Art. "Neo-Platonism."

that the relapse of the Pagan world into barbarism had nothing to do with the irruption of
untrained races upon the stage of history, but
was a necessary consequence of the intrinsic
exhaustion and abstractness at which the
ancient culture had arrived.

The facts are not to be denied. But, con-
sistently with them, very different modes of
conceiving the transition are possible.

The only definite set of phenomena which
I am at all qualified to bring before you are
those which concern the development of the
sense of beauty in the Hellenistic or Græco-
Roman age, which is commonly thought of,
from the standard of the greatest original art,
as post-classical and as a time of decadence.
Now this inquiry is very suggestive, for it
reveals to us in this period many elements of
modern feeling which are absent, comparatively
speaking, in the great classical art of Greece,

or, at least, of Athens. The delight in family life, the interest in man as man,[1] all phases of sentimental love, sensitiveness to the beauty of external nature, both in itself and as heightened by the contrast with city life, and by the idea of a historical or national " mission,"[2] and a new growth of literary sensibility displayed in the poetic appreciation of poetry,[3] all these things belong to the later age of minor literature and widespread culture and refinement within a great world-empire, in a degree unknown to the time when the greatest individual genius was concentrated upon the service of the commonwealths of Greece. So, again, the philosophers of the age after Aristotle, though

---

[1] Terence :—"I am a man, and nothing human is indifferent to me." Heauton-timorumenos, I. I. 25.

[2] Vergil, Georgic II. and Æneid VI. close.

[3] As in the conception of the Anthology or "Garland of verses" with the appreciative poetical introduction of Meleager.

by no means thinkers of the greatest grasp and insight, touch new sources of plain human feeling and simple brotherly[1] friendliness. Science, even, was advancing, at least to the end of the 3rd century B.C. The names of Euclid, Archimedes, and Apollonius (author of a Treatise on Conic Sections) are enough to remind us of this.

What was irrevocably lost to the ancient world with the liberty of Greece was the career for the individual man, the definite privileges and duties in which the ordinary citizen could express his personality and utter his will. In spite of this loss, much had been gained. The impression on my mind is very strong that Cicero and Vergil, not to speak of Epictetus, Marcus Aurelius, or Plotinus, belong to a world that has far outstripped the age of Pericles

---

[1] See Wallace's *Epicureanism.*

in ethical refinement and human sensibility, though inferior to it in energy and devotion, and in the conditions of individual greatness. The modern faults of pedantry and self-consciousness had appeared, and the new age was inferior perhaps to the old in the central qualities of moral life, while superior to it in breadth and refinement of ethical feeling. "Modernism," we must remember, had begun with Socrates and Euripides, while the distinction between this and the other world had been introduced into religious thought by Plato, together with the specific simile[1] under which the Christian Church often expressed the conception of visible things as symbols of the power and goodness of their Creator.

---

[1] Drawn from the relation of a father to his offspring, and sometimes further illustrated by the relation of the visible sun to its light, cf. Plato's *Republic* and Ep. to Hebrews.

Now it is hard to believe, without over-whelming evidence, that this broad and deep current of humane culture and emotion was suddenly turned back, or ended in a hopeless slough of evil.   As to the proportion of vice and corruption existing in the life of any time, direct evidence is exceedingly difficult to collect and to estimate.   We could make out pretty nearly what case we pleased either for or against the civilization of the present day. My contention, however, does not require me to suggest that we have in no degree improved when compared with the last days of Paganism. That would be a despairing view.   Yet when we pay attention to what satirists and con-troversialists tell us about the world as it was then, we should not forget what sort of case a preacher or a journalist can make out against us now.   Doubtless, a gladiatorial show was a more official, more murderous, and therefore more barbarous proceeding than any modern prize-fight.   Moreover, a prize-fight, in most civilised countries, is now illegal, whereas the gladiatorial displays—and other still more brutal displays of the same kind—were public festivals carried on before the head of the State.   Nevertheless, any one who has travelled in a great modern democratic [1] country when a prize-fight was about to take place, must have been surprised at the amount of attention devoted to it by journals and telegraph officials, and in the ordinary society with which a tourist is conversant.   We are inclined to say that our vices are at all events less coarsely proclaimed to-day; that a demand for purity and decency, at least in common social converse, has replaced the barbarity of

---

[1] I refer to a particular experience.   I do not mean to imply that a monarchical country is any better.

cultivated classes who could go together openly to such entertainments as those of the games. But as we speak of any such antithesis, echoes of a time not very long past come into the mind and deaden the opposition, while, on the other hand, in the private letters of Epicurus, or of Cicero, we catch glimpses of a family life, which, like our own, must have been to some extent a charmed circle, broken only at exceptional crises by the horrors of surrounding vice.

If we now try to frame some notion of the real junction by which Paganism is united with Christianity, we ought first to turn our attention to the immense lapse of time occupied by the transition. From the first distinct breach in naive or natural Paganism, to the assumption of a definitely doctrinal and orthodox form by Christianity, there is an interval which cannot be reckoned at less than seven hundred years, from the death of Socrates to the triumph of Christianity under Constantine; while, if we desire, as we ought, to consider the contact of the two influences as continuous down to the death of "heathen" philosophy, we should have to extend this interval to the closing of the schools of Athens in 529 A.D., bringing up the transition to a total of more than nine hundred years.

In place, then, of our supposing a chasm to have been suddenly bridged for the passage from Paganism to Christianity, let us make trial of a somewhat different set of conceptions. The age following upon that in which great discoverers have been active is confronted by the task of applying and popularising their discoveries, and often acquires, in consequence, a somewhat scholastic character. Scholasticism is in its essence the subordination of knowledge to practice, and in this widest sense our own time has, as I shall point out more in detail below, a scholastic tendency.

Now the classical Greeks had made the great discovery with which progressive civilisation begins, the discovery of a free and reasonable mode of human life; and this discovery they translated sanely, though not completely, into intellectual theory. But this discovery, like many new inventions, could at first be worked only on a small scale, and with reference to the very limited area in which the most favourable conditions existed. The same was the case with the monotheism and morality of the Jewish people, which in their combination as a moral religion were discoveries belonging to about the same period as that covered by the greatest time of Greek history. The task laid upon the succeeding ages was that of making available for the world at large these conceptions of an ethical monotheism and of a free but organised life. Especially the destruction of Greek self-government forced these problems upon the world, because, in the rigid machine of the Roman empire, there was much less fundamental moral distinction, than in a free commonwealth, between master and slave. And so among the Stoics, for example, it was possible for a slave to be a good man, and even to be a philosopher,—an idea which would have seemed profane to Plato or to Aristotle. The simple human virtues of the individual man or woman—the servile virtues—came to the front, and combined with the ideas of human brotherhood and of God in humanity, and also with that of a golden age in the future, perhaps the most important contribution due to the Jewish religion.

Thus, after four hundred years of struggling with these ideas in every shape and form, they were at last put in a popular and picturesque mould, and a new organisation was started to embody them in a visible society. So far, then, from being a new thing, contrasting with the degradation of the Pagan world, this great growth was the issue of the advance of that world during four centuries, and it was not thoroughly completed, in a definite shape, capable of ruling European civilisation, until, in a further development of five centuries, it had adopted from Paganism the germs of almost all permanently valuable elements that the latter contained. The five hundred years succeeding the Christian era were a time during which Christianity was still in the womb of Paganism, and drew its nourishment from the life and circulation of its parent.

The great need of the age, as is implied throughout in Professor Wallace's treatment of Epicureanism, was the need for a *practical* recognition of the individual human being, and a possibility of uttering his will in free harmony with his fellow-men. Ultimately, as we now see, the modern free nation was destined to replace the little Greek commonwealth in furnishing this scope and recognition, but in the meantime the Christian congregations served the purpose. In them every man and woman, independently of rank or station, found recognition, brotherhood, and hope. Now, this new hope and faith was simply the best ideal of Greece, translated, by help of Jewish imagery, into a coarse but popular shape. The advance, attended, as the law of such an advance rendered necessary, with a very considerable loss, was that it should be popularly accepted at all. It had needed four hundred years to get Plato's distinction between this and the other world into the popular consciousness; and when it did get there, it could only do so in the shape of a coarse material antithesis which showed and shows itself in the dominant understanding of Christ's " Kingdom of Heaven," just as it showed and shows itself in the dominant interpretations of Plato's " Doctrine of Ideas." Jewish aspirations, Stoic exaggerations, neo-Platonic dualisms, cutting life in two with an axe, were the instruments by which that naive and simply sensuous view of life, which Plato had rent asunder and re-combined in a rational whole, was finally rendered impossible for the European world. If this is what we mean by the exhaustion of a great life-principle, if to be exhausted is to be fruitful in the heart and mind of a world, which needs more ages than have yet elapsed to absorb the full significance of what has descended upon it, then, but then only, can we say that exhaustion and a relapse into barbarism were inherent in the development of ancient thought and conduct. The Dark Ages are not a proof that the great classical culture had lost its power for human welfare; they prove only how long a discipline was needed by the mass of humanity before it could appreciate more than the first stammering misapprehensions of its great inheritance. To frame this practical discipline, to impart the first elements of culture and dignity, not merely to new races but to the whole of those classes who had been within the civilised world but not of it, was the work of the greatest intelligences and characters of Christendom for a thousand years and more. Scholasticism, though it bears an external resemblance to speculation, has in it no true speculative elements.[1]   Its root is the sub-

---

[1] Scholasticism is a word with a definite meaning, and does not apply to all mediæval writings on doctrinal subjects.   In as far as there is true mediæval speculation, *e.g.,* in *Scotus Erigena,* it shows itself as a struggle towards a more free and complete view of life.

ordination of knowledge to practice, the attempt to find a bearing upon life in doctrines or tradition, not by grasping them as a whole, but by searching for an immediate application in every part.[1] Thus, that which all men could learn of the great ideas of Paganism was called Christianity, while as soon as they had learnt something, they necessarily gravitated back to a new and humanised Paganism. The first transition is symbolised by the images of Christ, which the Gnostics of the second century A.D. placed beside those of Plato and

---

[1] This view may seem to conflict with our received ideal of Scholasticism. Let us look at the doggerel verses which express its rule of interpretation, which even Dante accepts. "The letter teaches the facts, the allegory, what you are to believe, the moral" [interpretation] "what you are to do, the exalting" [interpretation] "what you are to hope." These are the four kinds of interpretation. The vicious predominance of practical aims in them is at once discernible. The whole labour and anxiety was to impress on ignorant men what they were to do.

Aristotle; the second by that painting of Raphael which seems to set heathen poetry under Apollo on a level with Christian doctrine under Christ.

The same relation holds in the history of art. The Pagan sense of beauty is not, as Matthew Arnold implies, destroyed in Christianity, but it passes into a form that included such elements of the older beauty as were suitable for this infancy of a new epoch with larger claims.   Naturally, among people to whom the arts of intellectualised imagination could not have effectually spoken, the first forms taken were those of architectural and decorative expression.   You cannot all at once raise a mass of slaves and barbarians to the intellectual life of Periclean Athens.   They remained for ages illiterate; but their sense of freedom and hope found its new expression in a shape that everyone could feel—the great churches with their decoration (often pictorial) and their services,[1] and we can see a more subtle sense of natural beauty continuing to grow from the first days of the Christian era. The history of art most strikingly confirms the point of view suggested above, that the popular mind was now grasping in a coarse and superstitious form, the principle to which Plato had tried to raise Greek thought. For the Christian consciousness repeated, on its own ground, an error of the higher Greek philosophy. In a great wave of feeling, about 800 A.D., partly under Jewish and Arabian influence, the Christian mind turned fanatically against all sacred sculpture and painting in the famous "iconoclastic" movement; that is to say, it felt for a time, as Plato had felt, that sensuous portrayals

---

[1] It is well worth while to read Mr. Pater's *Marius the Epicurean* on this whole subject.

appeared unworthy of and inadequate to the spiritual world. It was a mistake, but a mistake that could not have been made until Plato's conception that a spiritual world was a reality had in one shape or another penetrated the popular mind. And, of course, when a consciousness imbued with this conception should finally express itself in art, the result would be all the deeper for the discrepancy that had been overcome.

If, in order to bring the old and the new into close comparison, we look at the Christian consciousness by the side of that which is presented in Marcus Aurelius, the radical difference between the two is merely, I think, in the sense of hope or value in life. The Christian has, for every human being, the same sense of belonging to a spiritual body, which a Periclean Athenian had for himself and a few others. Only in the Christian this feeling is deepened by being generalised, and he considers himself to be of infinite value, as a member of a community in which the divine spirit is inherent. Marcus Aurelius has all the Christian sense of duty and goodwill and cheerful resignation, but it is conjoined throughout with an indescribable languor and weariness. We see it, so I cannot help thinking, in his face, the face of a weary man. And so there is something grotesque to our views, if also something noble, in the picture of the great general occupying the Senate with discussions on problems of philosophy for three days before departing on his last campaign. The same tendency shows itself in his favourite topic of comfort—that human life is so small a thing in the universe that our fate is really a matter of indifference. This consideration is not really helpful; and such world-weariness might, no doubt, turn to serious corruption in minds of a low order. All that was not getting better would be getting worse.

What was the root of this difference in feeling, explained in the language of philosophy? Clearly, the assumption of the self-sufficingness of the individual human being—the hopeless attempt to make the individual independent of an external response to his will. Plato and Aristotle, in conformity with the phenomena of Greek life at its best, start definitely and explicitly from the opposite of this idea—"society comes into existence, because each one of us is not self-sufficing but in want of many things."[1] The intermediate age of practical speculation had tried hard, in accordance with the isolated external life of the time, to escape this truth, but had only succeeded in making clear the individual's need, and revealing the impossibility of maintaining the inner will without an

---

[1] Plato's *Republic*, 369.

external organisation and reality corresponding to it. Plato's "righteousness" is the germ of Christian faith; the accepting as one's real self a purpose which is at once rooted in reality and represented by an actual society.

In the philosophy of the last age of Paganism there may be discerned a similar approximation to the theological principle of Christianity. Gradually the idea of emanation —that the derivative is the inferior—passes into the idea of evolution, that the derivative may reveal more than that from which it is derived. And the doctrine of Athanasius, by its insistance on the omission of a single iota,[1]

---

[1] Insisting that the Son is of *one* substance, "hom*o*ou-sios," and not merely "of like substance," "hom*oi*-ousios," with the Father. The point is, that the latter phrase leaves open the supposition that the Son, the medium of com-munication with man and the world, may have a lesser degree of divinity as compared with the Father, while the orthodox doctrine absolutely excludes this.

may be said to have vindicated the central principle of evolutionary science as the central principle of Christianity. The "give and take" between Christian and Pagan philosophy in this epoch was very considerable, and it is not possible, I believe, to judge from the purely philosophical writings of an author of the age in question, whether he should, or should not, be reckoned as a Christian. The tendency of the whole period, in which Pagan and Christian thought cannot as yet be firmly distinguished, was to begin the long task of reconciling the popular Platonic and Hebraic dualism by at least recognising that the good was capable of appearing in the actual life of man without deterioration.

When we look at this great historical development with ideas like these in our minds, it is impossible not to be struck by a parallel between the age of early Christianity and the present day. The Dark Ages, we are suggesting, were brought on by a new possibility and necessity for recognising the rights of common human feeling in virtue and art and worship, and universalising a certain inheritance of simple good, while sacrificing for the time almost the whole of the vast culture from which that good had sprung. Are we not forced to see something of the same kind within the area of our boasted universal intelligence of to-day? Let the dawn of the French Revolution and the outburst of ideas contemporary with it stand to us as the Christian era stood to the middle age. For the universal form of human feeling, which in that age ousted for the time being all regard to classical learning, literature, and science, let us substitute in our consideration of to-day the universal form of human intelligence, the membership of the republic of letters, the power and right to have an articulate opinion, to be heard in the court of science and literature, and in the argumentative deliberation which now rules the destinies of civilised mankind. Have we not, as a consequence of the great renascence of a hundred years ago, attained an advance which no one has rightly estimated, at the cost of a retrogression which no one has rightly understood? What we have attained is the universal right to argue, to have an opinion, to be heard through the speech on the platform, the book, the pamphlet, and the newspaper—the recognition that civilised man enjoys as his common birthright the form of articulate human intelligence. What, by this very advance, we have lost for the time, is the adequacy of the substance of culture to its form. Never before, in the history of the human race, have the facilities of thought and expression been so distributed as to render possible so wild and immeasurable an ocean of error. For positive error—and this is the simplest statement of my meaning—has now taken the place of ignorance. Far from having reached its climax, the movement towards a modern Dark Age has probably but just begun.[1] If early Christianity took on its shoulders the spiritual welfare of the masses in a very narrow sense, the nineteenth century has taken on its shoulders their intellectual and moral welfare in the very broadest and deepest sense. Do we suppose that this can be attempted without a sacrifice? Do we imagine that enormous benefits to the race can be obtained without paying a price? A glance at those countries where education, in the general or formal sense, is most universal and best appreciated, will assure us of the

---

[1] See some striking observations in vol. i. of Jowett's *Plato*, 3rd edition, p. 424 ff.

contrary. There is *nothing* which large sections of the educated populace (in all ranks of society) will not believe. There is no absurdity so gross as not to find its able journalistic supporters. There is no opinion which is not maintained, by persons equipped with full powers of articulate expression, with a granite obstinacy and indifference to reason and experience. There is nothing so bad in art and literature that it will not be welcomed with exultation by an enthusiastic crowd, quite capable of maintaining their conceptions in language, to all appearance, not unworthy of the republic of letters. Of this republic, I repeat, all civilised men are now in theory qualified citizens, and it wants but little for them to take up the external privileges of citizenship.

Is all this a ground of despair; and in speaking thus strongly am I a pessimist? I do not accept this inference. My object is to make clear that there is now a duty incumbent on all who believe in the organised substance of culture as a body of science, art, and literature, parallel to that which was laid on the advocates of Christianity in the Middle Ages, but at a higher level. Their duty, and their hope, lie, according to the point of view here adopted, in the direction of an ultimate reanimation of the form of culture by its substance. The so-called bankruptcy of the Pagan world was not its defect, but its merit. It had generated—so we may suggest—a universal need and a universal mode of feeling, which, because universal, were incompatible for the moment with the highest culture which had generated them, but were destined ultimately to combine that culture itself with something beyond. In just the same way the Revolution epoch has made known a universal need and formal capacity of an intellectual kind, but possessing, and likely to possess for many a long generation, only the form of intellect, and not its substance.

To illustrate the problem more clearly, an obsolete conception may be alluded to.   No one, it may be hoped, in addressing himself to an Ethical Society, would express a regret for the disappearance of authority in intellectual and spiritual matters.   But where there is no authority, we are badly off if the positive content of intelligence is wanting.   Authority, in these matters, may be defined as the influence of organised culture exerted by irrational means.   Now between the disappearance of this irrational influence, and the acquisition, by culture, of an influence operative through rational means, there is a transition stage which constitutes our peculiar modern form of the Dark Ages.   " Reverence," an able and intelligent gentleman from one of the British colonies once said to me, " is a thing I cannot understand." Well, the reverence of mystery is doomed ; the reverence of knowledge has not yet come.

To work for the completion of the universal form of intelligence by a content adequate to it is the next duty of all who have a faith in man's rational nature.

III.

THE CIVILISATION OF CHRISTENDOM.[1]

WHEN we try to embody in a characteristic phrase those central purposes which animate our modern moral life, there are three expressions that immediately spring into the mind. "Culture," "Humanity," "Civilisation," are the watchwords of the nineteenth century. In a romance written by Ivan Turgenieff, who was the prophetic voice of a slowly awakening people, we read the noble sentence : "My faith is in civilisation, and I require no further creed."

I wish to call your attention this morning

---

[1] Delivered at South Place Chapel, Finsbury.

to the profound and definite meaning which is really involved for us in these terms, which we employ so readily, without always bearing in mind their specific and particular force. It is a mistake to suppose that what is definite is therefore finite, or that what is individual is therefore narrow.   Nothing can be noble or infinite which is not definite; nothing can be broad or universal which is not deeply and pregnantly individual.   Which do we suppose has the more fertile content, and the larger comprehensiveness of relations—a logical formula that is true of all things and characteristic of none, or a distinct idea that sums up both for thought and for feeling the essence of some great human endeavour?

Especially in the chaotic condition of the age in which we live, it is to be desired that the main track of our advance, and the main outlines of our work, should lie plainly in our view, in order that we may not be blown about with every wind of doctrine, nor hurry to new superstitions wherewith to replace the old ; but that we may rather

> " Build to-day, then, strong and sure,
> On a firm and ample base ;
> And ascending and secure
> Shall to-morrow find its place."

I will comment in order on the terms which I have mentioned.

What is culture ? Is it to expose ourselves, passively, to the influence of all that men have thought and written, or are thinking and writing to-day ; to find all ideas and activities " interesting," and to maintain to them the attitude of the spectator and dilettante ? Oh, no ! Culture is the habit of a mind instinct with purpose, cognisant of a tendency and connection in human achievement, able and industrious in discerning the great from the trivial. Everything, no doubt, has a value, if rightly apprehended, but to apprehend things rightly we must apprehend them in due subordination. He who would be, or do, or know anything great, must have the penetration and resolution to limit and control his endeavours.

So too with the idea of humanity. We rightly welcome the saying of the Latin poet: "I am human, and nothing human is alien from me." Yet, if we ask ourselves frankly, "Does the import of humanity consist—*can* it consist, for me—in all human beings, past, present and future, with their wicked and wasted lives, and even with those lives which for my personal knowledge have had no existence at all, being of course the enormous numerical majority?"—if we frankly and candidly ask ourselves this question, the answer must certainly be negative. Humanity, as a moral idea, does not signify to us all human beings, actual in the present or past, and possible in the future, and is not in fact equally applicable to all human beings. And those who by a confusion of thought, together with an unguarded effusiveness of feeling, have wholly or in part imagined this to be the case—Count Tolstoi, if not misreported, furnishes an example of what I mean—have been led to turn their backs upon the noblest aims of humanity, and to counterwork its most essential purposes. To hear from a great teacher that intellectual culture must be renounced as a mark and cause of exclusiveness and caste divisions among mankind,—" Oh, the pity of it, the pity of it!" For, in reality, without culture there cannot possibly be any progress towards the solidarity of man as man. This sad error simply arises from not noting the distinction between the unorganised aggregate of human beings, and those definite coherent characters and achievements which alone give hope and value to life. It is the old, old difficulty of not seeing the wood for the trees, or again of not seeing the trees for the wood. Sentimentalism loves all human beings simply as they are; doctrinairism loves them only for the sake of the general purpose; rational enthusiasm loves them indeed as they are, but as seeing in them a relation to the general purpose.

A similar contradiction reigns in our idea of civilisation. Earnest and able men have pronounced civilisation a hateful thing; and it is certainly clear that not all the artificial life of wealthy and ingenious nations can enter into the idea which comes home to us as right and noble in the saying of Turgenieff's clear-sighted Russian. Let me read you the lines of our English woman-poet, which state this contradiction in a way, that, once realised, can never be forgotten. Mrs. Browning writes :—

                             " The age culls simples
With a broad clown's back turned broadly to the glory of
      the stars ;
We are Gods by our own reckoning, and may well shut up
      the temples
And wield on, amid the incense-steam, the thunder of our
      cars.

For we throw out acclamations of self-thanking, self-ad-
      miring,
With, for every mile run faster, 'Oh the wondrous, won-
      drous age !'
Little thinking if we work our *Souls* as nobly as our iron,
Or if angels will commend us at the goal of pilgrimage.

Why, what *is* this patient entrance into nature's deep re-
      sources
But the child's most gradual learning to walk upright
      without bane ?
When we drive out, from the clouds of steam, majestical
      white horses,
Are we greater than the first men who led black ones by
      the mane ?

If we trod the deeps of ocean, if we struck the stars in
      rising,
If we wrapped the globe intensely with one hot electric
      breath,

"Twere but power within our tether, no new spirit-power
  comprising,
And in life we were not greater men, nor bolder men in
  death."

These are words which it is right to bear in mind, as the question of the Sphinx which our civilisation must answer, or die. Our first feeling on hearing them is probably a combination of dejection at their truth, and indignation at their falsehood—so intermingled are the good and evil of our modern world. I cannot pass from them to my further suggestions without one remark, which is this: has there been any civilisation before or outside that of modern Christendom, in which so noble a trumpet-call could have been sounded by a woman?

These three expressions, then—culture, humanity, civilisation, are often superficially employed, cover dangerous bypaths, and need to be definitely interpreted.

Now if, in proceeding to define them, I were to ask of the more freethinking members of this Ethical Society the question which David Strauss embodied in a pamphlet many years ago, "Are we still Christians?" I suppose that the answer would be given without hesitation, which he also gave, "We are Christians no longer." If I were then further to ask, "Are we members of Christendom?" there would probably be hesitation, and the answers might be divided. If, finally, I were to ask, "Are we rightly described as heathens?" I should receive, I imagine, from all who think seriously, a peremptory negative. We feel, I believe, that though much in the Christianity of many churches is no longer intelligible to us, yet the mind and life of Christendom have gone through a process and reached a standpoint which makes *its* civilisation an essentially different thing from the mode of existence, however wealthy or refined, of non-Christian countries. I am not alluding to comparative statistics, for example, about soberness and chastity,—if any of the so-called heathen are really worse than we in these matters, they must be very bad indeed,—I am speaking about the whole nature and principles of fine art, science, politics, social action, philosophy.

Now, of course, it was not simply Christ's preaching that created the peculiar character of the western races, in which the constructive activities that mark our civilisation have their origin and source; but it is true, and cannot but be true, because the religion is the man, that Christianity was fitted to become and has become the definite and specific expression of the character of those races, which down to the present day have been the history-making races of the world. From the first it was a western religion, a Greek revolt against Judaism, becoming continually more and more pronounced ; and it embodied from the first, and under all its superstitions has never abandoned, those essential ideas which constitute the modern spirit.

The spirit of Christendom, then—parodied by its doctrines, but always animating its life—and the modern spirit are on the whole convertible terms ; and when we speak of culture, humanity, civilisation, as indicating moral aims and duties, we use these terms in the sense practically defined for us by the mind of Christendom.

At this point I think it not wholly impossible that I may be misunderstood. But standing, as I do to-day, in a place which has been for two generations a centre of free religious thought in London, I feel able to count upon a robustness of conviction in my audience which can afford to consider patiently the earlier life and traditions of a great religion. Our feet, I take it, are planted on the rock. It is nearly one hundred years since a great philosopher, in the dawn of what has been called the New Reformation, made use of the splendid words, " Our War-cry shall be Reason and Freedom, and our rallying-point the Invisible Church" (of all good people on the earth). And therefore, in the calmness of a free, natural, and rational conviction, we can afford to acknowledge the significance of the one great historical religion of the West in all its forms, without fearing to slide back into any kind of dogmatic superstition. Strength is brave and appreciative; only weakness is timid and exclusive.

Were not—I may be asked to begin with— were not the ancient Greeks and Romans great history-making races of the West, and yet were not they heathens ? and how then can

I assert that Christianity is the distinctive characteristic of the constructive Western mind? The answer is very simple : Christianity is the form in which the progressive civilisation of Greece and Rome expressed its tendencies when time and experience had partly matured them. Its first words, no doubt, were spoken by a heretic Jew from the despised northern borderland of Palestine ; but the actual shape of the new doctrine, as well as its effect, was determined by the thought and forces of the age,[1] and it is not perhaps in the genuine words of Christ that the Christian principle was most sharply or most profoundly expressed. So much by way of explanation. Greeks and Romans, in short, were not heathens in the full sense of the term. There would be a truth in calling them undeveloped Christians. Their lives and works are

____

[1] See p. 44 above.

bone of our bone and flesh of our flesh. They believed, as we do, that the revelation of the best for man lay in the eternal deed and purpose which alone gives value to the individual life. Their ideas are not alternative to ours, but belong to the childhood of our own spiritual race, and are already included in and operative throughout the spirit of modern Christendom.

What do I mean, then, by this spirit of Christendom which is, on the one hand the motor force of modern progress, and on the other hand the fundamental impulse of the new departure at the time of the Christian Era?

The modern spirit may be described as the spirit of rational freedom,—"freedom" because it fears nothing and acknowledges no superior; "rational" because it is not Stoic or negative, but positive and constructive. It not only believes that it can morally face the world, and even, if need be, meet destruction calmly; but it also believes that in fact the world is friendly, and kindred to itself. This, whether acknowledged or not, is the fundamental conviction of modern science, modern art, modern enterprise; although the progressive demonstration of it in detail, substituting itself for the vague faith in it in general, produces a curious and unjustified appearance of doubt. I cannot argue out this conviction at length. It is plain that we at any rate believe in no accident, no miracle, nothing in its nature and essence inexplicable or irrational. And not only so, but we believe that, whatever fate may be in store for the race, we can yet do, in spite of it, something worth doing.

In theoretical philosophy this point of view was formulated at the dawn of the New Reformation, just about a century ago, under

the name of the absolute standpoint. " Absolute," in this sense, means practically the same
as " modern "; it means that the universe is
not to be treated as a sealed book, but as an
open secret ; not, of course, in the sense that
we can, or ever shall, know all that we desire
to know ; but in the sense that we can attach
no meaning to the idea of something, which,
being particularly and especially of importance
for us to know, is yet of such a kind that we
are eternally debarred from knowing it. The
term "absolute" does not exclude relativity ;
on the contrary, its whole point and meaning is
that we have contact with and relation to the
reality of the universe. It does not exclude
a knowable relativity, but on the contrary
assumes it ; what it does exclude is an unknowable relativity. That is to say, it excludes
accident, caprice, and with these the vulgar
idea of the supernatural.

Therefore, I must point out, we shall be very cautious in employing the name Agnostic. Strictly, to be an Agnostic is to be a heathen, and we are not heathens, for we are members of Christendom. You will observe that Agnostic does not merely mean a man who is ignorant of many things which he would very much like to know. In that sense, no doubt, we are all Agnostics; but the great Agnostic writers have not spent their labour to prove anything so obvious as this. They mean more; they mean that there is something in particular of great and fundamental value, which somehow they claim to know and expect to know, and are disappointed by not knowing. This, I must confess, seems to me a ludicrous position; it perpetuates the prejudice which it professes to combat, and which is really a mere legacy, not so much from Christian, as from heathen superstition. Why are we, throughout

our whole life and work to stigmatise ourselves
as Know-nothings, if we believe, as I certainly
do, that what is best and most essential in the
world is accessible to our experience and realis-
able in our lives?   While admitting, then, that a
decent caution is wise and modest in describing
the range of our knowledge, I must point out
that Agnosticism, if it implies more than a
truism, implies what is incompatible with the
modern spirit, and is really a survival of the
worship of the unknown God at Athens, which,
in this one respect, was a truly heathen city.

Having thus described what I call the
modern or absolute standpoint, and having
illustrated it by its opposition to Agnosticism,
I go on to explain why I connect it in particular with Christianity, from which religion
it was in fact derived by the great men who
first proclaimed it in the time of Goethe and of
the French Revolution.

It may be said that the three teachers whose minds determined the future of Christianity— Jesus, Paul, and the writer of the fourth gospel, all believed in the existence of a personal God, dwelling in another world, which is the heathen doctrine darkly implied by Agnosticism, and especially incompatible with the modern spirit. And this is true; but let us examine the matter a little more closely.

In the foreshortening produced by great remoteness in time, the ages nearer to us occupy an apparent interval disproportionately greater than their actual duration. Christianity is nearly 1,900 years old, and we scarcely realise or take account of any similar lapse of time before the Christian era. But some civilisation can be traced for at least 3,000 years before the coming of Christ, and it is a very moderate assumption to suppose that supernatural religion, in some form, had existed for twice

as long before the Christian era as the interval
which has elapsed since that epoch. During
all this time, so far as we can possibly conjec-
ture, all reasoning nations must have believed
in gods, whose life was differently conditioned
from that of man, and interfered with his
capriciously, irrationally, and mysteriously.
This is the creed of a heathen. During the
last 500 or 600 years before Christ, the reasonable activity and intelligence of Greece and
Rome began to bring the idea of divinity
nearer and nearer to man, and to modify the
Judaic and heathen conception of the jealous
God, unapproachable by mankind.

And now, with this point of view in our
minds, let us turn once more to early Christianity. Unquestionably, the heathen belief in
the God in another world, or rather in another
section of this world, having existed, probably,
for 3,000 years, survived in the new teaching,

just as the custom of slavery, unquestioned throughout the same period, passed un-challenged into the new practice. But we do not judge a doctrine by its survivals, but by its novelties and ultimate tendencies. And the novelty, the new word, spoken faintly by Christ, but like a trumpet-blast by Paul and by the author of the fourth gospel, was this,— that God was revealed *in man*, that love and knowledge, the spiritual unity of mankind, were the actual being of God, so that ulti-mately the notion of Christ's second coming is transmuted into, and replaced by, this idea of the communication of *the divine* Spirit to the individual believer. Now, of course, the early Christian teachers did not anticipate how this new Christian doctrine of God in our world would, in the course of ages, crush and destroy the old heathen doctrine of God outside our world; but we, looking back, can clearly see how this conception of an immanent divinity, which is inherent in the character of the leading Christian races, has operated throughout their history as the organic idea. For, once more, the organic or evolutionary idea is at one with the absolute standpoint of the modern spirit. That a single principle or will lies at the root of nature, and is also embodied in the mind and actions of man, is the inspiring conviction of every progressive society, as of all science and practical energy. We can hardly realise the depth of the change by which this Christian doctrine initiated the belief in development, so characteristic of the modern world, unless we compare the timid social ideas of the wisest Greeks with the audacious metaphors which were the first that occurred to the Galilean peasant. How to avoid revolution; how to perpetuate the original wisdom of the founder; how to maintain a political equilibrium, the least derangement of which will be ruinous : these are the pre-occupations of Plato and Aristotle in their studies of society. But in the New Testament we have, at once, a different set of ideas. The use of organic metaphors must strike every reader. The operation of a ferment, the growth of corn or of a tree, are the illustrations that from the first occur to the speaker. Thus the future is quite differently regarded ; not as the painful preservation of equilibrium, but as a free and natural growth towards perfection. The reason of this is perfectly obvious ; it is that the revelation being immanent and continuous, will never be past but will always be present ; therefore there is no anxiety, the new principle can take care of itself, and, for almost the first time in the world's history the golden age is transferred to the future. Thus the first idea of the Christian is to convert the world, and we should reflect how modern this notion is; it rests on the conception of a universal humanity; no Greek ever wanted to spread Hellenism through the world; he did not believe the world was capable of it. The idea that humanity has a birthright, independent of race, and simply consisting in the one rational spirit inherent in mankind, is an absolutely modern principle, and lies at the root of moral and political progress.

The peculiar operation of this principle in Christendom might be illustrated in endless ways, from all aspects of action and intelligence. I will speak, not of its most fundamental manifestation, but of one which is the most readily verifiable, and was most undeniably peculiar to the Christian world. I allude to the history of Fine Art.

Fancy and ingenuity are present in the work of many nations, perhaps of all. But the art which deals nobly and reasonably with man and with nature is not, I believe, to be found, except in Christian civilisation, or in the Greek and Italian culture which was its forerunner. What little exception can be taken to this statement will only be found to heighten its force. We may remember that Mahometanism and Judaism alike prohibit the representations of plastic art, whereas the tendency of Christianity to representation and architectural expression at once reveals its fundamental kinship with Hellenism.

Facts like these are not accidental. The perception of the divinity of the human form, the sense of friendliness between man and inanimate nature (replacing the heathen sense of hostility), the demand that both dwelling-place and place of worship shall manifest the reasonableness and beauty of the spirit that lives in man, all these are consequences of the absolute faith with which the Christian consciousness claims to be in harmony with the world. We speak, sometimes, of the " Dark Ages," and in matters of the exact sciences perhaps they were dark enough. Yet we must deduct something from our youthful ideas of their obscurity when we find that our truest lovers of beauty fix the building age of the world between the years 500 and 1,500 of our era. Architecture, more than any other art, is an index to the happiness and freedom of the people ; and during this period of 1,000 years, "an architecture, pure in its principles, reasonable in its practice, and beautiful to the eyes of all men, even the simplest," covered Europe with beautiful buildings from Constantinople to the north of Britain. In presence of this manifestation of free and productive intelligence, unmatched even in ancient Greece and Rome, and utterly unmatchable to-day, we

may usefully reflect upon the expressive and
constructive force of the spirit of Christendom,
even in its darkest hours. The more closely
we examine the question, the less ground we
shall find for the conception of the Middle
Ages as a long sleep followed by a sudden
awakening. Rather we should consider that
ancient Greece was the root, and ancient Rome
the stem and branches, of our life; that the
Dark Ages, as we call them, represent its
flower, and the modern world of science and
political freedom the slowly-matured fruit. If
we consider carefully that the Christian human-
istic spirit held itself as charged from the first
with the destinies of the illiterate and half-
heathen masses of the European peoples,
whereas, neither in Greece nor in the Roman
Empire, was civilisation intended for more
than a third or fourth part of the inhabitants
of their territories, we shall not be surprised

at an apparent fall of intellectual level, which really meant the beginning of a universal rise hitherto unknown in the history of the world. Ideas of this kind may help us to understand what must remain after all a paradox, that we have been taught to apply the term " Dark Ages " to the period of what were in some respects the greatest achievements of the human mind, for example, the Cathedral of Florence and the writings of Dante. I am not one of those who can only appreciate the past by depreciating the present, and who show thereby that they have insight neither into the one nor into the other. But it is only right that we should throw off the childish prejudice that wisdom was born with us, and should understand that when we have done our very best with our opportunities we shall have done no more than is needed to prove ourselves worthy of the great tradition which we inherit. It is perfectly obvious now to all who look carefully at these questions, that the instinct of our physical science and naturalistic art, of our evolutionist philosophy and democratic politics, is not antagonistic to, but is essentially one with the instinct which, in the Middle Ages, regarded all beauty and truth and power as the working of the Divine reason in the mind of man and in nature. What a genuine though grotesque anticipation of Charles Darwin is there in Francis of Assisi preaching to the birds!

Now, while I do not on the whole recommend the use of theological phrases, I confess to being overwhelmingly anxious that we should not lose hold of this truth, which has never yet, as I believe, been *popularly* expressed without them. If we cannot say it without superstition, let us say no longer that human knowledge and art and morality are the continuous revelation of God. Only let us not imagine for one moment that man can either exist or be understood otherwise than as part of a whole, which includes inanimate nature as well as his fellow-men. Let us understand that the metaphor of the spiritual organism, introduced into ethics by Plato, and made by St. Paul the vehicle of his deepest teaching, is for us, as for them, almost the absolute truth. I will put it in this way. *If our only choice lay* between the doctrine of an inherent divine spirit in nature and in man, and the acceptance of the individual human being as no less isolated in the moral world than he is by his separate spatial existence in the physical world, then I should say unhesitatingly that the truth lay with the doctrine of the divine spirit. It is a plain fact that there is no separate moral reality precisely corresponding to separate human beings, such as I who stand here, or you who sit there. We exist, as animals, apart in space, but if our minds were wholly isolated and self-complete, as our bodies are, we should not be human or moral or reasonable. But all that is said of the divine mind remains equally true if we call it the best human mind. The difference is entirely one of words. The all-important truth is that we are only moral and human by finding a place in a system which is reasonable, which includes external nature, and which we did not make, and by transforming our separate animal impulses and desires in submission to a cause and purpose which we did not originate, and yet in which we can find satisfaction. Call it, if you like, the cause of humanity, but remember that the mere external look and figure of a human being does not constitute full humanity in this sense, though it does imply a capacity for such humanity. The difference between the individual who is possessed by this cause or pur pose, in the particular form which is demanded by his place and powers, and the individual who is not, is the fundamental fact which theological phrases are employed to express by men who have felt it strongly. The chief difference is not that between something in the world and something out of the world, but that between the man whose life is isolated as his body is isolated, and the man whose heart beats with the common purpose of humanity; and so deep is this distinction, that that which comes to consciousness in the spirit of man, being something greater than, and above any individual man, or any set of men, has, by many, been regarded as the awakening world-spirit or divine mind. We ought certainly to realise the weakness of ordinary language to express these tremendous truths. The more we reflect upon them, and the more, in the experience of life, our childish likings and caprices give way to the graver perception of the vast needs and possibilities around us, the more we shall feel that the language of Paul himself is not overcharged when he opposes the carnal mind, which is isolation and self-seeking, to the mind of Christ, which is the general will or spirit of united humanity.

We often speak with gratitude, as I have here spoken, of the great men and nations of the past, and of all that they have done for the human race. Am I falling into a too truistic vein if I ask you to reflect with me for a moment on the question—" Where is it all gone to ?" The poet says of the good that is past and gone, " Enough that God heard it once, we shall hear it by-and-by." But we demand a solution more relative than this. Some things, indeed, have a sort of permanence in ink and paper, on canvas or in stone, and on all this, if we have the mere decency to leave it uninjured, future generations may feed without our help or hindrance. But it is not in books and in buildings that the life of the past is handed down to the future; the mind of posterity is determined chiefly by such people as you and me.

Where, for example, is now that system of law which, I suppose, summed up the practical experience of the greatest practical nation through more than a thousand years, and culminated in the magnificent definition of justice as the constant and perpetual disposition to give to every man his own? Is it on the shelves of libraries that this national labour now has its reality? No; the Roman law lives to-day in the law-abiding will of the citizens of Christendom, in as far as they maintain their inherited and engrained disposition to give every man his own. We who are now living are the channels through which, and through which alone, the inheritance of humanity can descend to the heirs of all the ages. In as far as we are untrue to our trust, some result of human endurance is irrecoverably lost to humanity, some noble suffering is wasted, and those who come after us are defrauded of some portion of their birthright. Thus every ignoble application of time, every unworthy thought or act, is an irredeemable waste of something which was not ours to spend.

Of course, I know very well that the most useful men have often the fewest general ideas about their work. And certainly, if, for example, a man were engaged in building sound and healthy houses for the wage earners in London, I should readily pardon him for not troubling his head about historical Christianity or the civilisation of Christendom. Yet such a man, though unconsciously, would be influenced by ideas that are in the air, and by the spirit of his age. And if that spirit were, as we may make it, noble and enlightened, befitting the descendants of the cathedral builders, the dwellings that he built would be more likely to possess a little of that grace and beauty, which are so rare and so precious a boon to our labouring millions to-day.

And thus it is no more than right that, while doing in the first place our nearest and simplest duties with honesty and thoroughness, we should also, in the second place, keep our minds alive to the grand tradition of our spiritual ancestry—the tradition that human or Christian life is the full and continuous realisation in mind and act of the better self of mankind, that culture consists in the knowledge and active love of the best things, and civilisation in so arranging and performing our social functions that these best things may be accessible to all.

And it is in this sense, as the service of culture and civilisation, that we must interpret the service of humanity, the true solidarity of which must always be founded on reason. In the future a real unity of all mankind must surely come to pass; and the task completed by each race or religion will then be appropriated by the others. But while eager, wherever we can, both to learn and to teach, we must not abandon our own distinctive duties, but must carry out more and more perfectly that noble, complete and energetic conception of life which the growth of ages has developed as the civilisation of Christendom.

IV.

OLD PROBLEMS UNDER NEW NAMES.[1]

Is it well to revive the phantoms of a bygone day, which we suppose to be now at last happily laid to rest? It may seem a wise exhortation to "let the dead past bury its dead."

But we must bear in mind that if in one sense we have thrown off many burdens that belonged to the past, yet in another sense it is more to us to-day than ever it was to the mass of mankind before. For to us this present world is the theatre of our true life,

---

[1] Delivered at South Place Chapel, Finsbury.

and not merely its vestibule; and all that we are or possess in this present world belongs in its evolution to the historic past.

The first reason, then, for which I desire this morning to reinvoke some old enchantments that seem to have lost their force, is that we are men and women, and nothing human can be foreign to us. If we fancy that ideas, in which are crystallised the best men's strivings after the best through many generations, no longer have meaning for us, then there is something wrong with our hearts and our intelligence.

And, secondly, it would be as well that we should not get into a fool's paradise as regards the progress of the species. I believe that our ideas are definitely wiser and better at least in comparison with the cruder forms of theological superstition. But yet those underlying or overshadowing conditions of life and action which were represented in Christian theology still determine the possibilities of our entire experience; and though we may refuse to admit them as problems, we cannot for a moment escape them as facts.

And, thirdly, I almost hope that we are impatient of these prefatory explanations. If we of the ethical movement are anything, I suppose that we are lovers of the truth. And we ought not to excuse ourselves for spending half an hour now and then in a little voyage of discovery.

We will turn our minds, then, for sheer curiosity's sake, if we like to say so, to those two kindred ideas which represented for more than a thousand years the wisest men's conception of the universe in its inmost nature, and of our connection with it; the idea of an intelligent and beneficent Governor of the world, and of man's entire dependence upon the grace of God for the power to do any good.

1. The idea of an intelligent and beneficent Creator and Governor of the world has oscillated between two extremes—the personal and the impersonal—the notion of a will that can choose and originate, and the notion of a law, operative through the universe without choice or variation, although itself intelligent. I should fancy that almost every thoughtful child, brought up in the rigour of orthodoxy, has felt the pressure of the difficulties which are always tending to modify the first of these ideas in the direction of the second. The child is told that the Personal God is Almighty, and that right is right because it is His Will. Then, if God is Almighty, can He make what has happened not to have happened? Horace will confirm the schoolboy who thinks that this must be impossible. Can God make a

wrong thing right? If "no," there must be a law above Him; if "yes," right and wrong seem destroyed. Can God himself do wrong? If He cannot, has He that free will apart from which—the child is instructed—His own good action would be worthless?

Because of the continued pressure of these considerations it will be found that almost all the higher minds, whether Christian or non-Christian, are perpetually being driven towards the idea of divinity as a supreme law, which is expressed by comparing God with abstractions rather than with persons. "God is not a man that He should lie, neither the Son of Man that He should repent." "God is incapable of change or of evil; in Him is no variableness neither shadow of turning." "God is love"; "God is a spirit"; "God is truth"; "God is in and with those who believe in Him."

'God is law, say the wise, oh soul, and let us rejoice,
  For if He thunder by law, the thunder is still His voice."

But the view thus suggested no longer makes practical use of the personal will or intelligence of God. If a system of a certain kind is embodied in the forces of the universe, issuing, among other results, in the will and emotions of man, the purpose and intelligence of a Deity have nothing left that they can do. And so we find a further tendency to strip this supreme law of the attribute of a personal consciousness. I do not know, for example, if Tennyson's " Higher Pantheism," which I quoted just now, is intended to imply a divine consciousness or not.

Now, I am quite of opinion, that the assumption of a divine intelligence identified with the universal laws of nature in no way helps the explanation of the universe. But what I desire to emphasize to-day is equally true and far less familiar, and that is, that by rejecting the idea of such an intelligence we do not at all set aside the problem which used to be represented to us in that way; we merely set aside one mode of regarding that problem. The problem, or rather the significant fact—for I am not suggesting that it can be explained away—is that we are part of a huge system which we did not make and cannot control, and of which not only our bodies and organic sensations, but the ideas and habits which form the very tissue of our lives, are functions and elements. It does not much concern us whether or no this system has a separate mind of its own, but it does very greatly concern us what sort of tendencies are uppermost, or, whether there are any distinct tendencies at all in the great machinery of which human history is a portion and a result.

Now is not this in essence just the same condition of human life as that represented by the doctrine of the beneficent and intelligent Creator and Governor of the world? To my mind it seems to raise exactly the same question, with no change whatever except striking off a few accessory metaphors. I remember a young man at the University expressing himself as shocked and alarmed at the determinism involved in the claim of natural science to rational prediction. But it was asked of him whether he had not been brought up to believe in the divine fore-knowledge, and why this had not shocked him just as much. These two problems are in fact identical except in name, and so it is with the conception of a divinely ruling law and of a causal system.

Some people think that the argument from Design has lost all significance owing to the discovery of natural selection, which explains how the fact of adaptation, which produces the appearance of forethought, must necessarily arise under mere natural causation as we know it.

I am unable to see that this makes any difference to the fundamental burden of the argument from design, taken as simply relating to the nature of the causal system within which we find ourselves. To assume a creative intelligence does not help us; but to deny it does not help us either. I might compare the two accounts of design—that which supposes intelligent forethought on the part of a Creator and that which relies on the necessary operation of a causal system—to two modes of reproducing a decorative pattern which is incised or in relief. To take a pencil, and copy those lines which you want to copy, corresponds to intelligent design; to take a pencil and rub it freely over a paper laid upon the surface which contains the elevations or depressions of the pattern until they are mechanically reproduced by this process of rubbing, corresponds to design through natural selection. For the lines are in this case copied not because we pick them out, but because they pick themselves out by their physical nature.

"But I am assuming," it will be said, "that the pattern exists beforehand in raised or depressed lines." Now I will not insist that the adaptations in natural selection must similarly exist *beforehand* in the shape of causal conditions; the dispute becomes verbal at this point. It is enough to say that the causal system is such as by its necessary operation to produce the adaptations in question. This justifies my comparison, the point of which is that the one process is only somewhat more roundabout than the other. So far as the question is concerned, " What sort of system is it to which we belong ? " the two processes are on the same level for us. Not their method but their results are what concern us.

Of course, one accessory prejudice is finally shorn off by the discovery of natural selection. There is now nothing to suggest that the universe was arranged for the gratification of the feelings of every individual creature. But this was only a prejudice, and not a true inference, even for those who believed in an intelligent and beneficent Deity. We do not know enough to say that our happiness, as we from time to time understand it, would necessarily be the aim even of a beneficent Creator. The doctrine of eternal punishment probably served a useful end in balancing this ridiculous idea, and checking the notion that man's happiness must necessarily be the sum and substance of all things. The doctrine of predestination, again, allowing for metaphor, very fairly represented the fact. The system of things does condemn many persons, for no reason that we can understand, to savagery, or criminality, or at least to incapacity for the better part in life.

But whether we say that intelligence created the universe or that the universe created intelligence, makes no real difference as regards what we want to know. We want to know how far the universe is likely to respond to the needs of our consciousness both for practice and for theory. That it does so respond in some degree is the basis both of life and of science. And if it is cowardly to say on principle that there must be a compassionate Deity who will fulfil all our wishes, it is no less cowardly to assume in every minute and in every thought that our plans are reasonable and our knowledge of value, without daring to defend this assumption as a matter of principle.

I add one most striking illustration of what I mean. It is often said, " Design——conscious design—exists, and exists only, in the human will and in its products." Now, unless we are careful, we are here guilty of an enormous confusion. None of the greater results of civilised life are due to the human will in the sense of a single individual's purpose consciously entertained and pursued. All of them are due to an underlying relation between such purposes, which is a natural fact outside the consciousness of the individuals who cherish them, and belongs to the unconscious reason and providence of nature rather than to the definite foresight of man. No one man in history ever contemplated as a purpose the whole of what is contained in the British Constitution, the unity of the Italian kingdom, the science or philosophy of the nineteenth century, or the English language and literature. These products grew up, like a coral reef, by a relation of unconsciously concerted action between innumerable individuals, whose minds and intentions were determined in reference to one another by their historical position, birth, circumstances and education. Some understood and purposed more than others, but no one purposed the whole as it has arisen. The great constructions of human history considered *as wholes* are natural products, though in all *their parts* created by will and intelligence. No one in this room knows where in the nineteenth century his life work will be found to have fitted in. His purpose is to the general result like a brick in an arch, or, if he is a very great man, like a portion of the curve. The designer of the arch is after all nature, or what we used to call an over-ruling Providence,—whether conscious, or unconscious, does not matter to us a single jot.

Now I am confident that it is the conviction of a reasonable tendency in the universe that gives the modern Freethinker his strength as compared with the ancient Stoic or Epicurean, whom in many respects he resembles, but who had no working faith that anything great or good could practically be made out of the world, and who therefore relapsed into "saving his own soul" on a non-religious basis—a thing quite as possible, and to-day much more probable, than doing so on a religious basis. I do not contemplate with equanimity the reduction of our hope to that of keeping our wills pure in a hostile world. For, among other reasons, into the category of the hostile world would fall the conditions and generating forces on which we rely for all the larger human achievements. We are not strangers here on earth. Such a view would be a retrogression into the extremest superstition of a supernatural theology. I do not believe that ethical faith—faith in the reality of the good—is the spirit of a forlorn hope, though, if it were so, it would still be the only spirit possible for us.

But it is not my purpose to draw a moral to-day. My object was simply to insist that by dropping the notion of a person or of an in-intelligence, we have only shorn off some distracting accessories from the old problem of faith in God, which still governs life under the new name of faith in the reality of the good.

2. In the Catechism of the English Church, after instruction in duties towards God and towards our neighbour, the Catechism continues :—

" My good child, know this, that thou art not

able to do these things of thyself, nor to walk in the commandments of God and to serve Him without His special grace; which thou must learn at all times to call for by diligent prayer."

Many of us will be inclined to treat these words as unmeaning, on the ground that they imply first a libel on human nature, and, secondly, a miraculous remedy.

And we agree with any such critics that the spirit of man at its best is the best we know, and that we do not believe in miracles.

But is it really our experience that each of us, as he happens to be at any moment of every day life, is sufficient for himself? Have we never fought a losing battle against ill-temper, despondency, cowardice, or indolence? Do we seriously imagine that man's soul, the much-exercised mind of each separate person when most he feels his separateness, has be-

come, as Mr. Swinburne tells us, man's only
God? Should we not run the risk of justly
appearing ridiculous if we maintained this to be
so? If to admit the sinfulness of man were
enough for orthodoxy, I imagine that few of us
would be heretics. The old problem of the
conflict in man's nature remains a fact under
every new name. In the greater life of the
world, and more especially of mankind, there is
something which the animal individual may or
may not make his own, a principle on which he
may or may not lay hold, a direction in which
he may or may not set his face. Whether we
call it, with Plato, the ascent from the under-
ground den of ignorance and passion, or, with
John Bunyan, the Pilgrim's Progress from the
City of Destruction, is a mere affair of phrases
and metaphors. But if we think that the will
to be good grows up as a matter of course in
every man, and maintains itself in his mind

without help from a greater power than his, then we are in a fool's paradise, and have still much to learn from the Catholic Church.

These were the chief points on which I wished to speak a word of emphatic warning. When we read of God and Sin, we must not think complacently to ourselves that "we have changed all that."

But it is only right to subjoin a few words in order to indicate very generally what positive conception it now seems necessary to hold as regards man's helplessness and the means of grace.

i. In believing that humanity is sufficient for itself, we believe that though sin or selfishness are only too natural, yet a complete and energetic human life, which is also natural though not very common, involves a tendency to goodness. Although we do not think that to be good must always satisfy our human longings, yet there are some of these longings—for action, for self-development, for helpfulness—which are closely cognate with virtue. And even where the struggle is hardest, and the path narrowest, the striving is seen to be in the long run towards a fuller and more harmonious humanity, if not in every case for ourselves, then at any rate for others.

ii. It follows from this that the means of grace are no longer magical or limited, but are as wide as the influences which the greater world exercises upon the individual human animal.

In the first place, to conversion or regeneration, the birth of the spiritual man within the animal or natural man, there corresponds, now that the age of miracles is past, the whole process known as education in so far as it determines the normal frame of mind. The result of this process—a result which is inevitable, for he who is not well educated is educated badly—is to develop the mind into something which may be compared to a permanent though growing structure, in some ways analogous to the body. The parts and materials of this structure are ideas and interests, which are constantly reacting upon one another, and therefore upon the whole fabric. Some of them are what we call predominant or leading ideas ; they are more or less systematic, and therefore have a prevailing interest and form the backbone or framework of the mind. Others are more transitory, though not necessarily weaker in immediate attractiveness. Every idea has some interest, and probably, if left to itself, *would* produce action. But all real action issues, of course, from the whole state of the mind according as its parts or elements are influencing one another at every given moment.

Everything depends for the individual, first,

on the reasonableness, and, secondly, on the strength of the general framework or structure of the mind.   Do his dominant ideas represent a reasonable view and purpose—that is, do they grasp the larger or spiritual humanity,— and, have they force to maintain the balance of his mind against the shocks of life?   Heredity as well as education affect this issue; and both of these must be considered as the grace of the universe to the individual.   Fortunately, this grace is exercised in an increasing measure through the action of man.   But it remains startling, and I think ennobling, to see that each man's goodness consists, now as ever, in being the active incarnation of ideas that reach beyond his personal life.   I believe that I should convey most truly what I mean if I were to say, in the limited sense which the context indicates, that man's goodness consists in being effectually inspired by Divine ideas.

Some one may here be troubled by questions about the freedom of the will, which are exactly the same now that they were when man's liberty was thought to conflict with God's omnipotence. I can to-day only suggest in passing that in describing what is implied by human action we are not denying that man is able to act. For well known reasons a scientific description of any fact constantly sounds like a denial of that fact.

If education corresponds to conversion or regeneration, what is there in normal civilised life that corresponds to the prayer for grace? I should answer, in general terms, the openness to all influences which help the spiritual frame of mind, that should have been formed by education, to hold its own.

This openness may be described as a kind of reflection, though not all reflection is of this kind. It is a saying that those who deliberate are lost, and though impulse is probably more often dangerous than deliberation, yet reflection may mean perhaps at times only playing with sophistry. So I must designate the reflection of which I am speaking by the prosaic name of reflection upon reality. Its nature is clear from what has been already said. It is simply the process by which the mental frame maintains its equilibrium, and after or in spite of the shock of passion asserts its true position towards the larger world, as the needle points to the pole. Perhaps such reflection has more in common with the higher sorts of prayer than we are accustomed to realise. The essence of prayer was to bring two things into unison—the will of God and the will of man. Superstition imagined, no doubt, that prayer could change the will of God; but the more spiritually minded have always understood that the will which must be modified in prayer was the will of man. Prayer therefore, for us, or what I have not been afraid to call reflection, choosing the plainest language, however prosaic, consists in opening our minds in every way to the reality of the good. There are many instruments useful to this purpose, which it is not my place to enumerate to those who have more experience than I. Often where there is folly or temptation there is physical disturbance; food, rest, fresh air, a change of occupation, may be the remedies needed to restore the mental balance. Work is sometimes a safeguard; there is an old saying that he who labours prays. But the underlying reason for which all these things may be useful in their turn and in their degree is one and the same; it is the reinforcement of the spiritual frame; the restoration of control to those guiding ideas which link all sane life to the moral and physical order. If work, for example, is the specific, it is not because work hinders thought or deadens feeling, but because, being a pledge of the reality of the moral world, it diffuses a sense of this reality over the distracted soul.

"Are not," it will be asked, "are not human love and sympathy among the most powerful means of grace?" Doubtless they are, but, again, only as instruments. It is possible for them to be morbid or sentimental; it is possible for them to encourage vanity or foster selfishness. It is when they reawaken and reinforce the sense of a definite oneness with others, of a place which we hold in the human family with claims and functions laid upon it, that the emotions of love and friendship are able to do the work of saving grace.

Enough has been said to indicate the suggestion that I desired to convey. The overshadowing conditions of human life remain pretty much what they always have been. A reasonable faith and sufficient moral strength are now as always what we need. And for both one and the other we have to go beyond our separate animal selves, and to admit our dependence upon, while asserting our oneness with, the larger order around us.

V.

ARE WE AGNOSTICS?[1]

To begin with, is it worth while to talk at length about a mere name? Does it much matter whether we call ourselves Agnostics or not? This depends, I suppose, on the depth and clearness of meaning which a name possesses. And when we are not very far removed in time from the first origin of the name, it is likely enough that its meaning will be, in a popular sense, both deep and clear. For example, I do not know if there is necessarily much meaning just now in calling oneself a Christian; but when it might cost you your life

---

[1] Delivered at North Islington Liberal Club.

to do so, there was of course a good deal of point in this denomination.

Now the term Agnostic *is* of recent origin. It is not long since Professor Huxley, who claims to have invented it, explained in a magazine article,[1] why he did so, and what he meant by it. It seems that he belonged to a philosophical society, together with a number of eminent men of various theological opinions, and each of these persons had a denomination by which he could call himself such as Catholic or Deist or Unitarian, or whatever it might be. So the Professor, partly, I think, in jest, invented for himself the title Agnostic, meaning that he pretended to no knowledge or theories of a kind which claim to solve the problem of existence,—knowledge, that is, more especially, of a philosophical or theological kind, dealing

---

[1] See Huxley's "Essays on Controverted Questions," pp. 355, 356, cf. p. 331.

with the unseen or future world as conceived by theologians.

Now this is a pretty clear meaning, and it is also a somewhat deep meaning, because it implies that you think it desirable to take your title, and rank yourself in the intellectual world, according to your attitude on this question of a supernatural order of things. There are not so very many matters which we think important enough to name ourselves after in this way. Englishmen usually have a *political* name or profession of faith, Tory, Radical, or what not, and in the modern world generally it has become the custom to have a *religious* name or profession of faith—Christian—perhaps Protestant or Catholic—Unitarian, or Positivist. Of course this has not always been so with religion; I do not see how a man could have a religious denomination in ancient Greece or Rome; he might call himself a Stoic or an

C. C.   K

Epicurean, but I do not suppose that every one held any private opinion of that kind so strongly as to make him take such a title. I only want to point out that to take a denominational title of this kind is a step which implies a good deal. The title Agnostic, then, has a meaning made up of two parts.

1. It means that you want to call yourself by a name in respect of your attitude to the unseen world of theology—the supernatural, or, more broadly, the spiritual world. Because "Agnostic" does not mean merely "ignorant" in *general*: if it meant that, all reasonably modest people would be very willing to admit that they were Agnostics even about very important matters, and if the term may really mean "critical,"[1] about everything. But when

---

[1] *Op. cit.*, p. 362, Prof. Huxley seems to assign the word this meaning. But the attempt is not quite satisfactory; no one would give himself a special name, implying absence of

a man speaks for example of the religion of Agnosticism[1] he does not mean by Agnosticism our ignorance in general, but he means our ignorance of certain specific matters, which we used to be supposed to know; and these are, to put it shortly, what I have called the supernatural world, the subject-matter of old-fashioned theology. You have an opinion about this supernatural world, and you think this opinion so important, that you are prepared to accept a title or formula which indicates it. This is the first half of what Agnos-

knowledge, simply to indicate that he is faithful to the methods and limits which constitute knowledge. It is plain on reading the whole essay and observing the misused quotation from Kant (p. 354) that the author holds the lopping away of a spiritual world as conceived by theologians to be a more important aspect of thought than the recognition of that world within the range of human life by the greatest philosophers from Socrates downwards.

[1] Prof. Huxley favours no such conception. But it is a current idea, and as such may be examined.

ticism means, and it is because of this meaning
and this alone that I care to criticise it.   I am
not objecting to a man being an Agnostic in
opinion, but to his calling himself an Agnostic
in the sense that the name is to indicate his
attitude with reference to the spiritual world.
And here, as I judge from his phrase respecting " the problem of existence," *i.e.*, I presume,
the question what makes life worth living, Professor Huxley is Agnostic in the sense to which
I demur.

2. And the second half of the meaning consists in the nature of this opinion, which is
negative ; you think that nothing can be known
about the matter in question, and either you
are prepared to fight against the idea that we
can know anything about it—this is controversial Agnosticism—or you are prepared to *enjoy*
the mystery of the Unknowable, which is sentimental Agnosticism, and I suppose is indicated

by such a phrase as "the Worship of the Un-knowable." Speaking for myself, I *can* understand controversial Agnosticism, but I *cannot* understand sentimental Agnosticism.

However that may be, these are the two halves of the meaning of Agnosticism; first, you rank yourself according to your attitude on this matter; and secondly, your attitude is negative.

Now up to this point I have travelled the same road which is often taken by the modern defender of the faith. But at this point he is apt to execute one or two cunning gyrations which end by landing his follower, a little out of breath, in the old pathway of orthodoxy. I can indicate his track in a few lines of verse, borrowed from Arthur Hugh Clough in " The Shadow," a poem relating a dream that the ghost of Jesus came to the grave and declared there had been no resurrection :—

> " And English canons heard,
> And quietly demurred ;
> Religion rests on evidence, of course.
> And on enquiry we must put no force ;
> Difficulties still, upon whatever ground,
> Were likely, almost certain, to be found.
> The Theist scheme, the Pantheist and all,
> Must with or e'en before the Christian fall.
> And, till the truth seemed plainer to our eyes,
> To disturb faith were surely most unwise.
> As for the shade, who trusted such narration,
> Except, of course, in ancient revelation ? "

So long as you adhere to your Agnosticism, more especially if you try to make something out of it and so get into sentimental Agnosticism, so long you will go on finding that the pea has got back under the old thimble, and that instead of going forward into freedom you are back in the bondage of a heathen orthodoxy, worshipping the unknown God.

My purpose, then, this evening is to suggest another track that, in my opinion, it is time for us to take, so as to get clean away from the labyrinth of sophistry which lies around this frontier of the so-called unknown. I believe that the time has come to say in so many words that for us the Unknowable is and must be nothing, and that our business lies with the life and with the good that we know, and with what can be made of them. Agnosticism at best is self-defence, and little good work can be done while you are on the lookout for an enemy.

Now you would probably think it very odd if I were to say that Huxley and Herbert Spencer are in one respect like monuments of an effete orthodoxy. And yet, surely, nothing can be plainer than this, that we cannot lay the ghost of orthodoxy so long as we take our denomination even from our ignorance of the matters of orthodox belief. While you do this, you fix your eyes, not on the place where the spiritual world really is, but on the place where men used to think it was; and when your gaze is thus fixed on emptiness, there is always danger of hallucination. When I hear of the Religion of Agnosticism and the Worship of the Unknowable, I am haunted by the lines in Hamlet :—

> "Alas!   How is it with you
> That you do bend your eye on vacancy,
> And with the incorporal air do hold discourse?"

What I complain of, then, in the writings of these eminent men, in so far as they deal with the spiritual world or the world of reality, or the world above sense, is that there seems to me to be so little *in* them, so little attempt to grasp and put in organised form those chief positive realities by his apprehension of which man differs from animals, that is, is raised above the mere life of the senses. This *thinness* of doctrine is, I think, directly caused by the Agnostic attitude, and cannot give place to a richer culture until the attitude of ignorance is exchanged for an attitude of knowledge. An Agnostic may reply to this by saying that of course every negative is founded upon some affirmative, and that if we say we do not know the imaginary spiritual world, that is just because we do know the real spiritual world, the world of beauty, and goodness, and truth.

Now, if any one says that, I quite agree with him, and I only rejoin, " Has not the time come to make your affirmative explicit ; that is, to say, to the best of your power, what positively you do mean ? " It is the affirmative that wins, and convinces, and inspires ; why go on throughout a whole century protesting against exploded mistakes, till the new sermon becomes just about as dull as the old ? In this context I always think of Goethe's lines to America :—

> " Thou art happier, America,
> Than our old continent ;
> Thou hast no fantastic ruins,
> No castles torn and rent.
>
> Thou art not disturbed in heart
> At time of life's best fruit
> By idle recollection
> And profitless dispute."

If, as may well be, there is no longer any one connected set of doctrines which are to form the centre and pivot of our lives, why, then, I think, the time has come to say so, and to point out how, and in what more varied shape, human life inherits the great spiritual ideas and interests. My own impression is that our Agnostics have themselves to some extent lost their way, and that their delay in going forward proceeds from not precisely knowing in which direction to move. It is here that I wish to express a strong conviction, and urge a forward movement.

Never fear that life is likely to become empty. It has now all that it ever has had, and more. [The more experience we gain of great lives and great thoughts, the more we find that they all belong to the most real and tangible truths of every-day experience. Even imagination is greatest not by inventing the form, but by penetrating the substance. Always distrust people who tell you that the great men have despised this life and this world, and have said that there was no truth or reality to be found in them; distrust people who tell you that the basis of morality is something or other very deep, as if it was down a well, and had to be fetched up by philosophers; and in general, distrust people who try to make you believe that very important matters are to be looked for a long way off. This is the old trick of connecting faith with credulity, which Sir Walter Scott so wittily puts into the mouth of the German swindler. "Ah!" says Herman Douster-swivel, in the "Antiquary," "it is the want of credulity—what you call faith, that spoils the great enterprise." The identification of faith with credulity is characteristic of the knave, as that of imagination with falsehood is character-istic of the fool. Never believe that Paul or Plato or Dante or even Milton had it for their aim to remove men's thoughts and hopes to a detached and distant paradise. Their task was just the opposite—catching at the notion of a future and separate world, attractive to the human fancy of their times, they used it as an instrument to rouse mankind to the meaning of the world in which they lived. The future life, the happy hunting ground, is really an idea of heathen origin. The new and distinc-tive Christian doctrine was the future golden age *on earth*, and the revelation of divinity *in the human spirit*. And this depth of insight is the reason why, though the supernatural is gone from us, yet the nature which lives in the works of these great leaders will never cease to mould the hearts of men. And, as we all know, with Shakespeare and Goethe no such explanation is necessary. They are the *direct* interpreters of humanity.

So it always appears to me that of the two assertions which the term Agnostic implies the first is doubtful, and the second false.

The first assertion, that we need a name for our moral or religious attitude, is doubtful. It is not certain, to my mind, that there will be in future any doctrines sufficiently distinguished among the numerous important principles of human life, to make it worth any one's while to accept a denomination from them. Whatever has been true, no doubt is true, and whatever great motives Saint Paul or Saint Francis or Dante found in human life, exist, we may be quite sure, so far as they are truly noble, for us as for them. The long discipline of the past has not been thrown away. The law, Saint Paul said, was a schoolmaster to bring men to Christ, and the Christianity of eighteen hundred years has been a schoolmaster to bring men to freedom. I will not assert that we shall continue, as great men have proposed, to use the terms of orthodox religion, God, Worship, Immortality, with reference to the guiding characteristics of our purely human life. But we should be very foolish to suppose that the change of language involves a change of substance, and that we are to throw away what we have so painfully acquired, the knowledge of good and evil. We may now contrast good and evil as the true and the false self of man, rather than as the will of God in man fighting against original sin; but to a very great extent this is a mere matter of phrase and of language, and the essential fact remains, and grows clearer day by day and century by century, that in goodness a man takes up a spirit and a way of living which is greater than, and carries him away from, the easy-going purposes of his visible animal self, while it is only in wickedness or savagery that life even tries to limit itself by the calls of our sensuous nature. Does any man wish to see a far nobler miracle than the Resurrection,—not the recalling of a dead organism to life, but the elevation of an animal soul into membership of the supra-sensuous or spiritual world? *Then let him observe the education of his child.* The metaphors of old religion may now seem awkward and erroneous, but their language was not at all too strong for the facts which we *must* learn to see.

But yet, as we maintain to-day, we *have* learnt at last to read the facts of life without the guidance of rubrics and ceremonies and symbols. If this is so, I do not quite see where we are going to get our denominational or religious appellation, which would naturally arise from the rubrics or symbols that we might employ. I cannot well conceive that the civilised world will put its neck into the yoke of fresh quasi-religious societies, when it has once broken with allegories and looked plain facts in the face. We do not think any longer that there is any royal road to goodness, and therefore I can see no use in taking a name from our own special path.

For the sake of illustration, however, I will mention a movement and denomination in which many good people take an interest, and of which we here to-day are especially bound to speak with respect. If any one feels that he *must* have a moral denomination, and that he *must* have the sympathy and co-operation of like-minded people on a somewhat general basis, then he might find an example of the sort of union he requires in the Ethical movement.

The term Ethical is, I suppose, intended to indicate just that positive devotion to great interests of life, which the phrase Agnostic seems to miss. Its philosophical associations make it a little abstract and unattractive, and if it were construed to mean that the ethical philosopher was to be the priest or director of mankind, I can imagine nothing more degrading or more reactionary. But every term must acquire its meaning from its usage; and the usage of this term is simply to insist on duty and character, without insisting on any supernatural agencies or expectations. Time will show, of course, whether some such movement, or in some form a non-doctrinal Christianity, will be needed in the future by large numbers of people for strength and comfort. I do not myself believe it. In a time of transition, when, owing to the accidental conditions of the social medium in which we live, very many persons are unable to find the work and sympathy and the intellectual nutriment which they need, it is certainly useful to have a sort of directory of names by which people can be guided to that particular co-operation which they may require. But I look forward to the day when all these sects and societies and churches shall fade away before the more robust conception of enlightened citizenship. "My faith," as Turgenieff has said, "is in civilisation, and I require no further creed."

Then I do not believe that the first point implied in Agnosticism is to be accepted—that is to say, that we need a religious or moral denomination at all.

But, secondly, even if there is to be a religious or moral denomination, it will not be a negative one. The attitude of not-knowing is one which for good logical reasons the world is absolutely incapable of maintaining. The negation fills up as it is used, and the "not-this" expresses itself as a positive "that." What we want is a sympathetic study and perception of that greatness of our human past, which is continuous with the present, and is the foundation of our hopes for the future. I remember many years ago discussing with a friend the alleged necessity, for morals, of individual immortality. I had observed to him: "Surely it is not true, what they say, that one would think less highly of duties and affections if one believed they were all to end with death?" "Ah, no!" he replied; "how much more thoughtful and tender one would be for others, when one reflected that here was one's only chance, and neglect could never be atoned for." Something like this is true about the race as about the individual. The human past, present, and future are all that is ours, and of these the future does not yet exist, but is still in the making. Thus all our material of life, all we have to work with in constructing the future, lies in conditions and forces which are only known to us through the past, and our knowledge of which is itself among the forces. It is almost a terrible reflection that each generation of men is in turn the bearer of the cup into which has been poured the whole inheritance of mankind.

The very perception that this is so, that there is no supernatural omnipotence to replace our neglect of duty, is in other words a perception that the ideal is not apart from, but one with reality. And having apprehended this to be so, surely we shall go on from saying "the ideal is not apart from the real" to saying "the ideal is given in the real here and here and here." For positive effort, and strenuous effort, will always be needed to apprehend the ideal reality. I said, the reality is near us, is not separate and remote; but how hard it is to apprehend what stares you in the face. "A hundred men can talk," John Ruskin has said, "for one who can think, but a thousand men can think for one who can see." As we grow older, however, some little vision is forced upon us by suffering and experience. We learn the value of goodness, and of wisdom, and of the strong will. In our own efforts to explain how we feel that such and suchlike things alone are of solid importance, we can sympathise with the picture language of great teachers which neither the world nor they themselves have at the time found absolutely clear. We exclaim that goodness is the one real thing, wherever you find it; that the highest beauty, but not the mere stimulation of the senses, is the real thing to live and die for; that knowledge of reality needs patience and penetration; and that most men live in a world of indolent guess work and fancies. This is the sort of truth, partly burnt into even our common minds by long experience and persistent toil, which the thinker or prophet labours to impress upon his generation. But his generation listens with half an ear, and murmurs, " Oh, he is talking sheer metaphysics; he is saying that my enjoyment of my dinner is not a reality, but that General Gordon's character is; he is saying, too, that there is a real beauty which I am incapable of seeing—an obvious absurdity, for have I not a couple of eyes and an opera-glass? he is saying, further, that I cannot know anything about realities without labour and self-denial and patient practice in understanding, which is a scandalous idea, because I can use a dictionary like any one else." This is the sort of way in which people refute Plato.

I am trying to point out how much positive work there is for each of us to do. There *are* the two worlds; neither of them indeed supernatural, but both human; yet it was a far easier task to pass from a dream of sense to a dream of paradise than it is to pass from a dream of sense to the wakening of the intelligence. Therefore I grow impatient when I read about the world we do not know, and what a gain it is to us to realise our ignorance. " Good Heavens, sir!" I feel inclined to remonstrate, " do devote your acuteness to making clear something of value, to casting some light upon the past, or to unravelling some perplexity of the present." And I believe that the world is with me, and that whatever name, if any, it may take for its ethical banner, we shall soon have heard the last of Agnosticism. We all know

Goethe's famous outburst against the Agnostic
sentimentalism of his time :—

"They say," he wrote,—

> " Great nature's inmost heart
>   No human soul may know ;
>   Thrice-blest to whom her outward part
>   She condescends to show."

> " This cant I've listened to for sixty years,
>   And mutter cursing when it meets my ears,—

>   Nature has neither husk nor heart,
>   She shows her all in every part ;
>   But one distinction is eternal,
>   If thou thyself art husk or kernel."

One reservation, however, I must make, to
leave no doubt upon my critical standpoint. I
am, as I have implied, a man of peace, and
desire that we may devote ourselves, unmo-
lested, to the progressive work of the world.
But the most peaceable of men will buy a re-
volver if brigands are abroad ; and if, or in
so far as, we are still interfered with in our

peaceable endeavours by the " stand and deliver " of the obstructive, whether in education or in research or in any matter of grave importance to national or human welfare, then and so far I fall back on the position I had abandoned, and say, as a convenient close to discussion, " My good sir, it is no use, I am an Agnostic." It is a new way of becoming all things to all men, but is no less necessary at times than that which Paul recommended.

But I cannot conclude with such an admission. This old simile of a battle, drawn from Jewish ideas, and especially perhaps from the Revelation of John, and consecrated by the tradition of that very church militant against which we are apt to turn it to-day, is itself, more than any other orthodox idea, inadequate to the problems of the present. Intellectually speaking, there is something easy and indolent in a good stand-up fight. You have only to

say sharp and nasty things ; you are not
troubled with the most laborious of all efforts,
the effort to speak the truth ; battle is in fact
the acutest form of *mis*understanding, and frees
us from the human and intelligent labour of
construction, of organisation, of comprehension.
It is easiest to criticise, said one of the world's
greatest thinkers, harder to understand, hardest
of all to produce. The idea of a battle holds
up as virtue the foregone conclusion and the
blind persistence which make the picturesque
metaphor of an *army* so dear to every form
of superstition. With argument, as with the
sword, fighting is the resource of the man who
will not think.

The ideal of to-day is something nobler than
the battle-field. I was looking not long ago
at an old book which gave me many good
thoughts in boyhood — not a work of great
genius, but an honest and kindly English story,

"Tom Brown's School Days," by Thomas Hughes; and I came upon a description of a dream, in which one of the boys was supposed to have had a sort of moral revelation,—a dream that he saw all his friends and the people he knew about, among countless multitudes of others, all doing their part in some great work, and at last he seemed to see himself also, doing ever so little a part in the great work. This allegory seems to me to sound a nobler and more intellectual strain than that of "Onward, Christian soldiers, Marching as to war!" Patience, initiative, co-operation, comprehension, faith—these are the qualities of a man; and these are suggested to us not by the march against an enemy, but by the task which has to be contrived and adjusted in concert with others whose methods and whose capacities differ from our own. We do not here escape from dispute, nor even from quarrel and recrimination ; but it is the dispute and the quarrel of reasonable men who are divided in opinion about a process or a minor purpose, and who will not rest till they strike out a way by which their dispute may be decided *and their work may proceed.*

I think that, so far as I am concerned, very few campaigns in the history of the world would fire my moral imagination so effectually as the industrial enterprise, recently completed, of bridging the estuary of the river Forth. Those who have read the address on the subject delivered to a large audience of working men at Newcastle during the meeting of the British Association in 1889, must have felt the peculiar inspiration that springs from a constructive undertaking in which *all* have had responsibility thrown upon them, and *all* have acquitted themselves well.   It is not so much the distinguished engineer and the wealthy firm of metal workers who morally interest one, as the minor groups of mechanics who, working under new and most trying conditions, have displayed, as we are told, from day to day an extraordinary degree of courage, initiative, and contrivance.

Mrs. Browning has satirised our age as " Little thinking if we work our souls as nobly as our iron."   Would it have been too captious a question to put to the poetess, if one could have asked her, " Is it possible to work our iron nobly, and not in doing so to work our souls nobly too ? "   It is true, however, that not the value nor the weight of metal, but only the human character in-wrought in the structure can give it nobility to the eye of reason ; and it is thus understood—as a monument, that is, of courage and of reasonable co-operation—that any such gigantic mechanical undertaking may serve as an allegory of the moral enterprises before us.

Let us then, taking example from the bridge builders, consider our life in the light of a positive and reasonable organisation of interests and purposes.   Let every man, living to begin with in the duties of an honourable citizenship, seek out for himself and for his circle the most rational adjustment of conduct, and the highest interests, which come within his view.   And if he chooses to busy himself with the history of opinion—a most worthy and human subject of study—let him always ask himself not "how much can I condemn as having been false," but "how much do I inherit that is true ?" remembering that he is accountable to posterity for the material which is handed down to him. Some knowledge of this kind is helpful to moral faith ; all men do well to learn something of the wider mind of humanity.   But if such study meant a condemnation of the past and a complacent embracing of our own empty denials, then it would be a worthless study; and it would be far better to plunge into the present, and merely to learn by the direct experience of to-day.   In either case, whether through historical insight and sympathy, or merely through the experience born of high aims and reasonable endeavours, we shall be able to forget our Agnosticism, and to say with Goethe,—

" How wide is my inheritance, how spacious, how sublime,
  For time is my inheritance, the field I till is time."

VI.

THE COMMUNICATION OF MORAL IDEAS AS A FUNCTION OF AN ETHICAL SOCIETY.[1]

THIS is a subject which has been much discussed in private among us, and when it was suggested that there should be lectures upon the work of an Ethical Society, I thought that it might be profitable, one evening, to interchange ideas on this most difficult aspect of our operations.

It is in great part a practical question, and is very ill-fitted for dogmatic treatment; and in dealing with it I feel more especially the truth of what a friend observed to me the other day.

---

[1] Delivered at Essex Hall for the London Ethical Society.

"You know," he said, "I think all preaching has a certain affinity to bad manners." Then, on the other hand, it is of no use talking at all unless one speaks pretty freely; so I wish to throw out quite boldly the suggestions that present themselves to me, and to illustrate _them as distinctly as I can, just in order that people may think over such things, if what is said comes home to them; and if not, they can pass it by.

Everything is contagious. We are all of us always communicating ideas, and more especially moral ideas, and it might be said that an Ethical Society could exist without making any *special* attempt in this direction by platform utterances or by teaching the young; it might exist for various classes of useful work, or as a federation of more limited organizations, united only by the actual definite sympathy of fellow-workers; and by such an existence it would still, through its work, be communicating moral ideas.

But the ethical movement has had from the beginning a point of view which its members have been desirous to communicate in a more or less general form. And, perhaps, assuming that the existence of societies with so wide a purpose as that of the ethical movement is in itself desirable, it is further inevitable that the attempt to communicate moral ideas should take, among other forms, that of teaching or of lecturing ; otherwise, the comprehensiveness of the ethical purpose might perhaps destroy cohesion, for no purely practical organization can effectively maintain so extended an aim as that of promoting good life. A benevolent nobleman, who lent his house for many philanthropic purposes, used to exact from every visitor a contribution of one shilling for the " Universal Beneficent Society." This idea was always and properly ridiculed. You cannot have a practical society for improving things in general. Practical operations must form each its own organization, and if you want to retain in unity a number of separate working branches, then it may be desirable to make some attempt at expressing and communicating such moral ideas as represent the spirit of your action. Objections may be raised against any form of words, and it has occurred to me sometimes to doubt whether the term "ethical" is wholly free from ambiguity, when taken to indicate the concrete, though ideal, purpose which we of the new reformation recognise as our common property. The word has an appearance of alluding to "ethics" or "moral philosophy" in a way which I am obliged to deprecate on theoretical and practical grounds, which the present lecture will, I hope, make plain. But those who have the capacity to initiate a movement have the right to christen it ; and any one whose petty scruples about the use of a technical phrase seem likely to deter him from co-operating in his degree with an effort which has substantial value should, as Aristotle would have advised him, "listen to what Hesiod says," in lines which I should like to see set up as a motto in all places where men meet for action and deliberation,—

> "Supreme is he whose wit meets every need,
>   And good is he who wise advice will heed ;
>   But he that cannot teach, nor will not learn,
>   He is a fool that no man's wage should earn."

We now have this ethical movement, which evidently meets a certain need. It has brought us together, and we therefore think it desirable not merely to work, but to utter here and else-where, in plain language, for the furtherance of our purpose in coming together, such matters as may best promote the spread of an enlight-ened morality.

How, then, not merely by example and by ordinary civic activity, but by teaching and lecturing, are moral ideas to be communicated?

I will begin by considering three kinds of suggestions, which I have gathered from private communications, and from observing what is actually attempted by various agencies.

(1) One friend, who permits me to refer to a conception on which he has expended much patient reflection, has formulated a scheme for bringing together the best heads of all civilized nations, to consider salient questions or cases of reflective morality, their judgment upon which should then become public, backed by their authority, for the improvement of the general standard and of the general practice.

Now, I will not urge, as a final objection against such a scheme, that authority is destructive to free morality, in which every man must be his own tribunal, because my friend

only intended that the precepts to be thus formulated should come before the world with a
certain weight, entitling them to consideration.
And this, of course, would be a perfectly fair
use of moral influence.   But I will say at once
that I feel compelled to conclude that a further
form of this same difficulty would be fatal to
the conception, in the precise mode in which it
presented itself to its author's mind.   It presupposes, I think, that morality is a sort of
separate district or province of life, in which
some selected persons, or eminent pundits, are
more especially at home.   But this suggestion
is abhorrent to me.   Morality, as I think of it,
is a way of living.   And therefore it is not
certain, in the first place, that even the simplest
decisions or verdicts could be universally valid;
for duties vary with the conditions of individual
lives.   It is certain, in the second place, that
no really difficult cases could be embodied in

such decisions; for every conflict of duties is a unique question of the shape and growth of a particular individual life, and no collection of thinkers can put themselves in the place of one man, much less of every man, so as to tell him, " Thus and thus your life must be shaped." All attempts at general guidance of this kind are and remain platitudes. The great satirist Rabelais knew this when he depicted a man asking advice whether or no he should marry. At the end of every sentence in which he states his case, as his wishes vary, and the colour of his statement varies with them, his interlocutor's advice alternates between, " Well, then, marry," and " Well, then, don't marry ! " through several closely printed pages. Most of us, I think, who have asked, or who have given specific advice, will recognise the portraiture.

But do I say, therefore, that there is nothing

in the conception upon which I am comment-ing? No; I think there is something in it. When such suggestions are made to one, I think one ought always to look round and ask one's self, " Now, is there anything which has been actually done to which this idea should direct one's attention, and what conditions of possibility do the actual facts suggest? " And if we hold tight to the truth that morality is a way of living, and that important questions of the way of living are important questions of morality, then we find that international con-ferences do take place on grave moral matters with valuable results. International arbitra-tion, international copyright, the labour and short-hour question, the suppression of the slave trade, primary education, poor-law, and charitable administration,—in all these pro-vinces, and many more, the experts of different nations have held intercourse, and have done much to arrive at reciprocal enlightenment and a common ground of action.

Now, what are the conditions of these useful and effectual deliberations ? Clearly, I think, in the first place, a special tribunal or conference for each kind of questions ; and, secondly, as the essential reason for this condition, a previous habituation of the assessors, by work on common lines, or by the pressure of a common and definite necessity, in entering into one another's lives.

It is not, then, that the members of the conference are to be regarded as moral pundits, and that others come to them for the resolution of specifically moral cases ; it is, rather, that one man or woman is toiling, say at infant schools, in London, and others at Naples, and in Berlin, and in New York or Chicago, and all these can come together consciously to good purpose, because, in the bonds of a common work, their lives were already united. Let me take one homely example. Ask your chorus of pundits, "Is it moral to break down the responsibility of the parent for the sake of a direct good to the child?" I cannot predict the answer of such a chorus, but one thing I can say with absolute certainty: it must begin with an *if.* "If the good to the child is genuine, does not undo itself, can *only* be got by the sacrifice of parental responsibility, and so on, then——" What on earth can such a reply tell any reasonable creature that he did not know before?

But now let us suppose that we have a conference of managers of schools, together with experienced poor-law or charitable administrators. Let us take the history of family after family, analyze it, observe the effect of free dinners and of self-supporting paid dinners, both on the family and on the neighbourhood, and then let us—do what? Pass a resolution on the matter? Yes, if we like; but, chiefly, let us go back to our work and shape it as best we can, not necessarily in the same mould all over the world, but in the light and in the strength of the vital moral experience which, by others' help, we have now made our own.

I think that this condition of a definite common work or common necessity, shared by those who are to decide, and relevant to the question to be decided, gives us the type and limit of what is useful in moral decisions by experts, and of the persons to whom alone such a decision can be of value,—namely, those who share the common experience in question.

(2) On the other hand, a question has been raised, how far abstract philosophical matter should enter into the communication of moral ideas. All that I have to say to-night is in

answer to this question in its most general sense, but in a more specific sense I will try to give it an immediate reply. It is taken to mean, I think, "Are we to go into problems, say, about the nature and existence of the Deity, or about the place of consciousness in reality,—theological or metaphysical ideas,— with a view to demonstrating something that may make in favour of morality?" No; as a rule, I think not. We must not suppose that the foundation of everything is somewhere outside the thing itself; and we must not suppose that the supports of any moral theory are the supports of morality. Unquestionably, moral philosophy involves a good deal of metaphysics and psychology. But it is possible to present a reasonable view of moral facts without explaining all the metaphysical ideas that such a view may ultimately be found to imply. I may compare the relation of intelligent morality to abstract philosophical doctrines with the relation of the species and genera of plants, as naturally classified, to the most universal laws revealed by physiological research. The two subjects are intimately connected, and you cannot explain how the plants came to be what they are without knowing profound and ultimate physiological facts, which, at the present moment, no one can be said to know. But this does not make you doubt that a fuchsia is a fuchsia, and is cognate with a willow-herb, or that wheat is a grass which has become by cultivation one great basis of human life. And so with morality. It is undoubtedly interesting, and may be instructive, to pursue by analysis those implied truths or general facts which lie behind the existence of man as a moral being. But a reasonable view —a right arrangement according to affinity and value—of the facts of human life can be presented without metaphysical formulæ, though *not*, in my judgment, without the analysis of human society, of the chief interests of life, and of the temper known as ethical faith. For these are not outside morality, but are its constituent elements.

(3) If we do not call œcumenical councils of morals, if we do not discuss theological or metaphysical problems, ought we, however, in our teaching, to advocate ethical ideas in the sense of abstract ideas about morality, such as the principle of " justice," which we hear of a good deal to-day, or the " ethical principle of economics," which finds its way at times into ethical programmes ?

As a help to considering this question, let us think for a moment about the distinction between a science and an art.

A science has knowledge for its purpose. The subject-matter of a science is single, coherent, and shaped by an inevitable logical growth. An art has practice for its purpose; the matter with which it deals is many-sided, and falls in the province not of one, but of many sciences, from each of which the art borrows, without any rule beyond practical necessity, such information as may throw light on the particular cases submitted to it.

An art deals always with particular given cases. A science cannot deal with a particular given case as given; it demands, like a superior court, that the case should be stated, and answered hypothetically, assuming the truth of this general or hypothetical statement. Therefore you can no more go straight from ethical science to social or economical practice than you can from physiological science to medical practice. We all saw, but the other day, how ludicrous in the eyes of an illustrious physiologist appeared the notion entertained by an abstract thinker that medicine was the deductive application of physiology.

There may be, or might be, an ethical art related to ethical science as medicine to physiology. The art of the catholic director of consciences was intended for an art of this kind; and in a lesser degree it is one, no doubt, which in going through life we all exercise, well or badly. What in such an art we especially need is experience of life and insight into the particular case before us. "I wish," a friend may say, "to provide allotments, at my private expense, for the labourers of my native county; is not this well?" "How good of you; how altruistic," the ethical scientist must reply, if he is fool enough to judge from the case as laid before him. But it may be that the ethical man of art, who knows a thing or two, might rather feel impelled to ask, with some suspicion, "Were they not saying something about your standing for the county next year?" A timely question of this kind is about the best that ethical art will do for us.

But, to be serious, I do feel obliged to speak strongly upon the direct application to life of abstract formulæ. When I hear of its being a question of "justice," how much a man should be paid *per* hour, or how the land of the country should be held, I feel a positive sense of horror. I *know* that nothing can result from such a point of view, except that any forthcoming prejudice or superstition is withdrawn from reasonable criticism and embodied in a fanatical creed. The superior morality of a form of land-tenure or of a special economic arrangement seems to me a superstition which precisely takes rank with that of the divine institution of private property. I have seen somewhere, in these discussions, the phrase

" abstract justice." If ethics has a word to say on the subject, it is that abstract justice is a very well-chosen formula to express what is necessarily unjust. Justice is a concrete, the condition produced by a reasonable organization of society. Plato ought surely to have taught the world thus much in two thousand years.

Speaking generally, then, I am strongly of opinion that to confuse ideas about morality with moral ideas is a very dangerous thing. I would never, for example, tell people that there is a standard which they ought to follow, and a sanction which they ought to value. As a general rule, perplexities of conscience are avoided by living out one's own life and attempting always rather to enlarge one's point of view organically than to vary it capriciously.

Thus, taking ethical ideas to mean ideas

about morality, and moral ideas to be leading ideas in life, I should direct myself to communicating, as a rule, moral ideas, and not ideas about morality.

I am very well aware that in an intellectual age this distinction is not absolute, but the nature of science makes it certain that the distinction will always exist.

The idea, for example, that it is especially desirable to feel good, or to feel bad, is an idea about morality; the idea of a particular good thing to be done is a moral idea. Any formula of justice, such as equality or merit or need, is, standing by itself, an idea about morality; the conception of some definitely possible good life is a moral idea. The idea that self-sacrifice is virtuous is an idea about morality; that conception of his particular task for which a man will "scorn delights and live laborious days" is a moral idea. The idea that the will is free

when the man is good is an idea about morality; but the will can only be liberated by the
apprehension of particular moral ideas.

Ideas about morality, then, are the abstract
or scientific renderings of moral ideas. They
have value both as an element of the great
fabric of knowledge, which is one of man's
characteristic achievements, and as a clue which
may help us in framing a distinct and organized
conception of our moral environment. But we
do not adequately realize that the clue is not
the organized conception, and may even be a
hindrance to it. The way of methodic science
is a long way, and its half-way houses are un-
satisfactory. Many and many a soul has died
of spiritual hunger in the midst of spiritual
plenty, because these aids to vision prevented
him from using his eyes. The result of all
science and philosophy is to see things as they
are, and he has done himself a very evil turn

who has gone up into the abstract world and has not come down again. " I suppose you mean the great philosophers," it will be said. Oh, no, I do not; they know their way in both worlds safe enough. I mean the small philosophers, such as we are ourselves, when, in our very aspiration after the general form, we lose our hold of the particular substance. I do feel that in this ethical movement we are not free from this risk, which has been the pit-fall of what is commonly known as Christian philanthropy. To the general aspiration, " I want to do good," the first answer is, " Then live out your own life thoroughly and intelli-gently." It is right in one's leisure time, or if one has no peremptory private duties, to find a sphere for work such as ours in guilds and schools and lecturing. But I most earnestly believe that the fault of the present time is, on the whole, distraction, and that one great cause of this distraction is the notion of a general duty to do good, as something other than and apart from doing one's work well and intelligently. Now, do we not think, if we are honest with ourselves, that in reforming or preaching or volunteer teaching, or making schemes for moral crusades, we are doing something of a higher class than is done by those hard-worked ordinary persons who teach for money in schools and colleges, or organize or practise industry, or write books and newspapers? Well, I say no; it is they, and those of us who work like them, who carry the world on their shoulders, and the moral atmosphere of whose endeavours is the true medium of the communication of moral ideas. And if, in talking about doing good, we divert our forces or our insight from our own work, and allow this to have the sin of haste and imperfection, which by universal consent characterizes the work of to-day, then I say that our ideas *about morality* have become an absolute hindrance to our apprehension of *moral ideas.* I will not labour this point longer, although every year I feel it more and more strongly. I will sum it up simply in a question. Are we quite sure that we give due ethical importance to thoroughness and intelligence, which involve finish and organization, in ordinary work, when it appears careless or even contemptuous of the stock-phrases of morality? Do we quite realize, for example, how, for all educated persons in the world, the idea of duty must have been deepened by that most cynical but splendidly laborious of historical writings,—Gibbon's " Decline and Fall of the Roman Empire " ?

Is there any way, then, by which moral ideas, as distinct from ideas about morality, can be directly communicated ?

How can *ideas* be directly communicated at all? We often think communication much easier than it is. I take an example which is a very extreme and a very striking one. Money, in the shape of actual coin, is readily transferable. We are therefore apt to think that those things, for the sake of which we desire money, are transferable no less readily.

This gives rise to what experts call the carcase theory of benevolence. There, we think, is the mass of well-being; you have only to cut a piece off and give it to the first comer, and it will be well with him. Not at all; you can do nothing whatever of the kind. In giving him money you are applying an external stimulus to his life. How that life will react to the stimulus depends upon itself. Practically, it may be said, you cannot transfer even money,—that is to say, you cannot certainly transfer the normal and ordinary benefits which we associate with the possession of money.

And if it is hard to transfer money, what must it be to communicate ideas? Not to discourage us, but to elevate our notions of our task, I want to be allowed to say freely what I feel about this.

What is an idea? An image, like a photograph, that you can take out of a box when you hear its name? No, I do not think it is at all like that. An idea is a complex but definite habit and effort of thinking; to apprehend an idea requires, in varying measure, courage, strength, practice, skill, and, above all, patience. If we sometimes compared the task of communicating ideas with such tasks as teaching a man to skate, or to run a mile in four minutes and a half, or to sketch from nature, we should be saved from some at least of our errors. The reason why *I* cannot use

the differential calculus is, on the whole, the
same as the reason for which I cannot play the
violin.   Both of these activities require skilled
and sustained effort of a kind which I have
never learned to make, and which now, probably, I could not learn to make.   Luckily,
not all ideas are as hard to grasp as the calculus, and not all efforts need, like the
musician's employment, a very special bodily
endowment.   But all ideas whatever present
difficulties of apprehension such as are presented by these.   An idea is a portion of life,
and you must not hold it cheaper.   The carcase
theory of knowledge—the theory that ideas are
stowed away in a sort of bank and it is stingy
not to distribute them—is as common and as
fatal as the carcase theory of well-being.

And, then, a " *moral* idea ! "—that is, a set of
familiar facts thoroughly grasped and realized
in a point of view which makes them a leading

interest in life,—that *is* a hard thing to communicate. Contagion, I said, is always communicating moral ideas; and contagion, perhaps, after all said and done, remains the only certain way.

Aristotle says somewhere, in one of those crushing sentences that make one doubt whether it was worth while to live after that great man, " It is one thing to repeat the formulæ of knowledge, and quite another thing to possess the knowledge." I think we sometimes suppose that moral ideas have been communicated to us when they have not. I am not a revivalist preacher; but the test question, to ascertain whether we have or have not apprehended moral ideas, is pretty much the same that such a preacher would ask his congregation if he wanted to know how their souls were getting on. What can one do now that one could not do before? Does one enjoy better books ?   Does one care more for true thoughts or for beautiful things ?   Has one a deeper hold of one's civic or neighbourly duties, of one's family or parental responsibilities, of one's humanity as embodied in one's daily work ?   If no change of this kind has taken place, then one may have been much interested or excited, and may have participated in a certain ethical dissipation, but one has not apprehended any moral ideas.   " Active impressions," said Bishop Butler, " by being repeated, become stronger ; passive impressions, by being repeated, become weaker."   The terms seem incorrect ; but the sentence expresses a fact.

However, we do not want discouragement, but encouragement ; so reminding ourselves, in another Greek saying, that " great things are hard," we will approach the problem itself with the help of a comparison or two.

I spoke of a difficult mathematical idea, that of the differential calculus. None of us here, if we have not been trained in the subject, would find it at all easy, or worth our while in later life, to apprehend that idea in a workman-like way. Nor, again, should we for the most part be justified in devoting the time and labour which would be needed to make us thoroughly expert political economists or thoroughly competent biologists. The ideas of mathematics, of political economy, and of biology must, therefore, as systematic and complete ideas in these sciences, remain, as a rule, beyond our reach. But if we ask whether mathematical or economical or biological conceptions are wholly without meaning for us, and without influence on our lives, why that, I think, we should deny. Helmholtz, Clifford, Mill, Jevons, and Darwin have very deeply influenced the intellectual life of our age, and half directly and half indirectly of all of us here. We have learned from them probably not so much as we think, but certainly something. They, or others following them, have applied their great ideas to the organization of experiences which come home to us, and to the definition of relations which lie within our ken. Some one, perhaps, has even demonstrated to us some simple physical relations of sound, or some contrivances tending to self-preservation in a plant, or the statement and refutation of the antiquated wage-fund theory. And, besides this, all our experience in daily life is unconsciously organized or crystallized in new shapes, embodying and revealing the new points of view as they gradually permeate life.

We may thus form some guess, I think, what sort of thing to aim at and to expect in the communication of moral ideas.

I must interrupt myself here to recall what

I said about contagion. The talker is, I think, very much more likely to get moral ideas from the busy men he talks to than they are to get them from him. But we agreed to assume, this evening, that there is to be talking, and the only question is how it may be made most useful. And we must remember that the talker or teacher may be of use, if only by interpreting back to his hearers those very moral ideas which he has gained from them. Moreover, it will be seen, from what I am going to say, that the most useful teacher for our purpose is not so much a man of abstract theory as a man of reasonable experience. Theory also, of course, is one work among others.

Now, in throwing out suggestions about our function in the way under discussion, I want to put before us what, in one sense, though not in all, is the hardest case. Let us assume, as it was suggested to me by some remarks of Dr. Coit that I should assume, that our audience consisted less than it does of reflective and leisured people, and more of men and women whose lives permit but little book-learning and are hard throughout and liable to extreme hardship. Have we, it was asked of me, anything to say to these? Is not the Statement of the Society to which I belong (Report, p. 1), " The good life has a claim upon us in virtue of its supreme worthiness, and this claim is the highest it can have," easier to people who have from time to time a spare afternoon and a spare shilling, which in modern London means a good deal of enjoyment, than it is to those who never attain this combination of resources? And is it not still harder, if they have at times to see, in those dearest to them, an artificial want and suffering in excess of the ordinary ills of life which we all have to endure as we may ?   Have we, in short, a message for the many as well as for the few ?   I might be interrupted with the outcry, " These things ought not to be borne, and you should not persuade people to bear them."   To this I answer with an old Scotch proverb : " He that *tholes*, overcomes."   (" He that endures, overcomes.")   The spirit that endures, as a man and not as a slave, is the spirit that conquers.   While the world lasts, patience will be the foundation of courage.

Well, then, we are not going to tell them about a pleasant future life, nor about a special interposition that will help the good in distress. Our experience is quite different from that of King David, who had never seen the righteous forsaken nor his seed begging their bread. Yet candour compels me here to blunt my rhetoric by saying that genuine righteousness, on the whole, does not *tend* to beggary.

Is an ethical maxim, that worthy life is sufficient for itself, real and helpful for the many? Would you go into the cottage of the poor family, whose father and breadwinner had just been killed by an accident, and read to them out of our programme that "the good life has a claim upon us," etc.? or, if a man in the thirteenth week of a strike came in here to listen to us, would you expect him to be much edified?

Let us try to look at this matter neither cynically nor sentimentally, but with the truth of both these moods, and of our own standpoint. We are not to forget that "fine words butter no parsnips," while we are also to remember that in trouble, as in humble station, "a man's a man for a' that." I mean that he has in him something strong and sympathetic, which dies hard even under crushing misfortune.

Should we then begin reading No. 1 of our statement of principles to any one in hardship or in distress ? I suppose not. I imagine that our own principles would forbid it. Morality is life, and you cannot plant a strange life in a man by force, and all in a moment. As Plato tells us, you must make it grow from within.

First, then, just because our method is true and not false, it is slow, and ought to be begun in time. Everything is curable, O. W. Holmes has said, if you call the doctor soon enough ; but "soon enough," he continues, might be two hundred years before the patient's birth ; and people seldom fetch the doctor so soon as that. I admit that it is harder for *us* to pacify "the first strong burst of anguish," in a mind wholly new to our ideas, than it is for one who has at command the wonted anodyne. We look to moral prevention rather than to moral cure, and to moral cure rather than to moral anæsthesia.

But, secondly, as I have tried to urge throughout, our work is based upon our principles, but does not consist in giving our principles as pills. What is our most general principle? I suppose, from our statement, it is the sufficiency of humanity. What is our duty, then, to the suffering, the ignorant, the unleisured? Why, I suppose, to enter into their lives and to make their own humanity appeal to them. Even respect and natural human courtesy do something; contagion, I repeat, is the real thing. Honest and intelligent sympathy does more, and does so much that I almost retract, as regards our most gifted workers, what I admitted above. I am acquainted, I think, with persons of our opinion, who, never for a moment tampering with the truth, would be as much valued in any sick-room, or in face of any calamity, as the best provided minister of soothing illusions. A sensible person, if sympathetic, is always a rock to lean upon. At least, that is my experience.

Thirdly, much of the accustomed form of consolation is even now quite unreal. The ministers of religion are generally good men; and it is largely the good man's unconscious humanity, and not the form of its expression, often wholly unintelligible, which comforts and strengthens. I note one further point : his official position makes him the representative of the general sympathy. A strong consciousness of solidarity is needed to compensate for this feeling. For most of the poorer class in our town, however, the accustomed form of consolation is already known to be value-less.

But passing from these most extreme cases,

which always demand some special qualities in those who deal with them, and in which the sufferer is destitute of the reasonable habits of mind which give solid human strength, let us think of the more general question, "What message have we for the working man or woman?"

The general form of the answer must be that which we have given above; our message, as we deliver it, cannot be the *idea about morality*, which is expressed by saying that humanity is sufficient for itself; it must be rather those moral ideas by which, in the various ranks and phases of life, humanity is made to feel and to be in very truth sufficient for itself.

I once asked a great philosophical teacher, "Am I not right, sir, in thinking that you are influenced by the categories of Hegel"? "Yes," he replied, "they are very useful things;

but one need not tell everybody that one uses them." He was not thinking of any concealment, of course, but merely of not puzzling people with abstractions. And so, even if you use ideas about morality, you need not show them except to such people as may be interested to see them. What *must* be communicated is a point of view worked out in life, and in some particular form of life which those whom you wish to help will recognise as their own. Take as an example the modern ethical doctrine of the freedom of the will, which I may state broadly in the abstract form, " A man is free when he has found himself in his moral environment." To make men and women realize this cardinal condition of their humanity, you must not talk about *it*, but you must talk about the facts in which it has its truth *for them*. I should think that if, as I hope, the parents of some of the little children in our

Infant School come next week to see what goes on there, *they* would receive some elements of the organized view of life corresponding to this "idea about morality." That is to say, they would see, and perhaps be told, in simple language, by ladies to whom this education is a heartfelt reality, how the child is being helped to grow and act, and in growing and acting, to be spontaneous and yet orderly. Even marching to music is, in its degree, and for young children, an object-lesson in moral freedom. It is finding satisfaction in doing a thing rightly, finding yourself in the order of the world. I know very well that people do not take in these ideas all at once. Rome was not built in a day. But let them once be interested, and they will soon catch hold of the free and happy humanity that is brought out in their children. And of course the whole of life can be treated in such a way as this, and, moreover, its range can, though most gradually, be extended.

But, above all things, the knowledge and experience must be real and vital. You must not take it into your head to illustrate free will, and get up the subject of infant schools to do it with. That is scamped work, and must produce a bad moral impression. You must have really entered into the faith of the sufficiency of humanity in that particular form in which you were to treat of it. And then, gradually, the organized life which forms your moral ideas will grow up in the minds of those with whom you are in contact, and then, "though he fall, he shall not be utterly cast down." For they will have laid hold on reality, on the true value of life.

The fatal home-sickness of the Swiss or the Scotch Highlander, touching and romantic as it may be, is ascribed, not without justice, to the simple singleness of his hold on reality. The single root is cut, and the tree withers. A man's power of endurance is measured by the depth and fulness of his life, and it is the communication of such a fulness in the shape of moral ideas—that is, of intelligent interests —which constitutes, I suppose, our message to the poor.

Need the ethical teacher himself have reflective ideas about morality? My own conviction would lead me to answer in the negative. Thorough moral ideas, in some department of life, are the indispensable condition. Truth agrees with truth, and a reasonable man, with sound experience in important matters of knowledge or of practice, will be able to communicate something of the order and grasp of his own moral organization. Any one who has had the good fortune to be gradually trained in some complex perception, as, for instance, the perception of beauty, by the teaching of other minds more gifted than his own, has a fair example of the process which I understand by the phrase, communication of moral ideas. It is not to create new things; it is not to dig up hidden things; it is merely to open our eyes and hearts that we may see and feel things as they are. It is incredible, I think, to the very young or inexperienced how the pictures in a gallery, or the poems in a book, gradually through long years, as our point of view becomes truer, are transformed from mere paint and canvas, and words and rhymes, into living meanings and spiritual symbols. Just so, and just as incredibly to those who think they see already all that common life can show, do the simple and familiar facts of life change their perspective and their grouping and their value, and become instinct with significance, and grapple us with an ever-new reality.

For my own part, then, I feel no hesitation whatever about the question that was put to me. What may become in the future of any particular society I do not know. But that moral ideas are the essence of humanity, and can be *awakened* to consciousness *in*—this is a better phrase than *communicated to*—all in whom humanity is still alive, I entertain no shade nor shadow of a doubt. Nor do I doubt that the condition of success is to envisage life in its fulness without sacrificing its organization, so that to all sorts and conditions of men their own humanity, which alone can do them good, may be interpreted. From the nature of this work it is plain that mankind cannot, as one used to think, be saved by one man nor by one society. All that we can do is to take the portion of work or of teaching that lies within our individual range and try to make it thorough and reasonable. Patience and thoroughness

are, I think, the chief watchwords in the communication of moral ideas. Failure generally
means indolence or superficiality or narrowness.

What we are to do, I take it, is, in the first
place, to live our own lives out solidly and
rationally, and, in the second place, to procure
such utterances and such teaching as naturally
arise from reasonable and energetic minds
thoroughly versed in the various relations of
humanity. And so living and so teaching,
whether in or out of an Ethical Society, we
shall be communicating moral ideas in their
true form as growing germs of life. And although I am no advocate for quasi-religious
proselytism, or for the multiplication of new
societies, yet I see clearly that in the interval
now before us, until a free humanism shall
become the spirit of the civilized world, it may
be well for men and women to band themselves
together in holding up the banner of such a

humanism for the help and encouragement of the isolated. And undoubtedly in so doing it may fall to their lot, by plain sense and true-heartedness, both of word and deed, to bring reasonable activity and reasonable faith within the reach of courageous spirits struggling in solitude. This is a meaning which might be found in those splendid verses that draw the moral of Goethe's Faust, putting into the song of the angels in paradise something more appropriate to plain men and women on earth :—

> " We rescue from the evil one
> This spirit high and brave ;
> Who still aspires and labours on,
> Him we have power to save."

There is no magic in the matter, you see ; every soul must save itself ; but between it and others there is no unfathomable gulf, and life, like everything else, can be communicated. We have to see to it that the life which we are communicating is solid and sound. Half-culture, half-insight, half-devotion, half-conviction are the insidious enemies of our work. The spirit in which moral ideas have their being, and by which alone they can be communicated, is expressed in the familiar motto of the "strong, much-toiling sage," whose name I have just mentioned :—

> " And I vowed it, then and there,
> Vowed all halfness to forswear,
> In the whole, the good, the fair,
> Resolutely living."

VII.

RIGHT AND WRONG IN FEELING. [1]

THERE is a right and a wrong in matters of feeling. And, strangely enough, it is more easy to obtain an assent to this assertion with regard to art and literature than it is with regard to life.

First, then, we will speak of the easier case, and after that, we will apply ourselves for a moment to the harder.

No one denies, to-day, that there is a right and a wrong in the feeling that embodies itself in art. Moral right and wrong, indeed, we do

---

[1] Delivered at Prince's Hall, for the London Ethical Society.

not predicate of poetic or pictorial sentiment;
but none the less, we recognise, though in a
wider significance than that of morality, a something that is sound or unsound, gold or tinsel,
great or contemptible, in the emotional qualities implied by all that pretends to be beautiful.
It is not to our purpose, to-day, to consider the
precise relation between the æsthetic and the
ethical "right and wrong." It is clear that
they are not the same, and that in æsthetic
criticism the mere moralist is a pedant; but it
is no less clear that in æsthetic feeling, as in
everything else, duty commands us to be right,
and not to be wrong. Just so, morality has no
rules for building a bridge; but if we are to
build a bridge, it is a matter of morality to build
it aright.

The incalculable importance of beauty in the
education of the young arises from this simple
fact, that it is the primary and unmistakable

example of a right and wrong in feeling. For the young must be trained by feeling ; and it is a great thing if they form the early habit of discerning that in all emotion there is right and wrong.   In this way the grasp of the objective is laid from the first upon the whole of life; and that vicious habit is averted which regards the domain of sentiment as something upon which reason has no possible claim.

How vicious this habit is, we may learn by considering the nature of feeling or emotion.

For feeling or emotion appears to be the peculiar echo of the individual organisation upon the occurrence of ideas or of sensations. An abstract idea is, or pretends to be, the same for all ; my triangle is your triangle, so far as our intelligence is what it should be ; but my emotion is the particular echo of my personal being, like the response of the piano-strings, when permitted to vibrate freely, to a complex tone impinging upon them. My emotion is not your emotion, unless my whole being were your whole being also.

Thus to exclude feeling from the dominion of reason is to deny that the personality of the individual can be modified or permeated by intelligence.

Feeling which is concerned with beauty, it should be observed for distinction's sake, is disinterested feeling ; that is to say, though personal, as existing in us, it is not personal in the sense of being concerned with our private purpose or desire. It is the echo of a contemplation and not of a volition.

I now select, to represent respectively the feeling which is rational and the feeling which is irrational, the two connected terms, "sentiment" and "sentimentalism."

"Sentiment" is, no doubt, a neutral phrase, and is frequently employed in a disparaging

sense.   But as sentimentalism is always so employed, I propose to retain the term sentiment
to designate a certain justifiable sensitiveness,
the nature of which I am about to describe ;
while by the term sentimentalism I shall indicate, conformably to usage, that kind of
sentiment which is unsound or tawdry or contemptible.

The word " Sentiment," then, may rightly be
used to denote that quality of sensitiveness,
e.g. in art and literature, which peculiarly distinguishes the modern world.   Schiller's tract
on the naïve and the sentimental is practically
a treatise on the differences between classical
and romantic literature.   " The poet either
is nature, or seeks nature."   The former is
naïve or classical, the latter is sentimental or
romantic.   This distinction has been variously
applied ; but in any case it has the merit of
drawing attention to that peculiar yearning for

a response on the part of nature to human moods which is at the root of romantic feeling. Sentiment, in this meaning, though readily distorted, cannot be banished from art. It may be described as sensitiveness to all signs of unity between man and the world. An interest in the beauty of nature, Kant has told us, is an index of a good mind ; for it implies an interest in the unity of things—in the response of the world to human or moral ideas. Healthy sentiment is the emotion generated by such an interest or such sensitiveness. It is alive to suggestion, but is innocent of distortion. It retains the full sanity and clearness of the intelligence, and even while white-hot with passion allows nothing to obscure the fact. Such is the sentiment even of Homer and especially of Dante. When Homer's Ulysses, —I draw the example from Mr. Ruskin's treatment of the Pathetic Fallacy—when Ulysses is startled by finding his friend (whose death was unknown to him) in the land of departed spirits, how simply he addresses him :—-

"Elpenor, how did you come under the shadowy darkness? You have come faster on foot than I in my black ship."

Contrast Pope's translation—

> "O say what angry power Elpenor led
> To glide in shades, and wander with the dead?
> How could thy soul, by realms and seas disjoined,
> Outfly the nimble sail, and leave the lagging wind?"

The "nimble sail" and the "lagging wind" are mere conceits, implying a frigid and false reflection, wholly inconsistent with the hero's eager enquiry.

Again, "when Dante describes the spirits falling from the bank of Acheron, as dead leaves flutter from a bough" (I quote from Ruskin), "he gives the most perfect image possible of their utter lightness, feebleness, passiveness, and scattering agony of despair, without, however, for an instant losing his perception that these are souls, and those are leaves; he makes no confusion of one with the other. But when Coleridge speaks of—

'The one red leaf, the last of its clan,
That dances as often as dance it can,'

he has a morbid, that is to say, so far a false idea about it; he fancies a life in it, and will, which there are not; confuses its powerlessness with choice, its fading death with merriment, and the wind that shakes it with music."

True sentiment, then, is the echo of the healthy personal individual frame to an idea or perception,—a response which does not confuse or distort the apprehension of that to which it responds, and therefore is not antagonistic to depth and truth of insight, but intensifies these qualities, and is in turn intensified by them.

Sentimentalism is different. It is not a

single-hearted response to an idea or perception ; not the direct echo of our personal frame,
however sensitively tuned, to the stimulus impinging upon it.   It is a response to the excitement of responding ;   an echo artificially
sustained for the pleasure of the sound.   Like
the voluptuary, whose desire is directed, not
to an object such as other men desire, but to
the pleasure that may be had by stimulating
desires in order to experience their satisfaction,
so the sentimentalist has his interest, not in the
significance of an idea or perception, but in that
excitement of feeling which the idea has power
to arouse in him.   Feeling as such is pleasurable, even though its content be of a painful
nature, as Homer tells us by the phrase
" enjoying the chill lament," and as Burke has
pointed out in analysing the delightfulness of
grief.   To feel for the pleasure of feeling is
then the note of sentimentalism ; and in the last

resort, it is much the same disposition of mind as that of a man who drinks because of the heightened interest in himself which springs from the excitement caused by drinking.

Now the point of the problem lies in the relation of sentimentalism to the idea which is its object. Mere emotion, as common language indicates, is closely connected with mere sensation. The sensation-novel is a production directed to afford the reader the pleasure of emotion, without subjecting him to the effort of apprehension. It must have occurred to every lover of stories that the actual incidents dramatised by Æschylus and Shakespeare, or narrated by Scott and Thackeray, are often no less startling in their nature than those which in a common-place romance are rightly set down as sensational. But common language is right. A sensational novel or picture is rightly called so, not, however, because it gives us strong sensations, but because it gives us mere sensations. A great critic in commenting upon a popular novelist once observed, "She used only to draw propensities, now she draws characters." The craving for emotional self-indulgence is incompatible with that exaltation of the faculties which accompanies the spectacle of a profound passion or character strong to dare and to endure in the face of realities. Such a craving distracts the attention from the core of ideas, and sends it wandering through the bypaths and the accessories, where feeling may be most cheaply bought. The experienced novel-reader knows too well, when the grammar is bad, the observation of nature superficial, and the reasoning childish, that there will be a gloating of sentimentalism over trivial things, and a coldness of genuine sentiment towards the deeper issues of life and character. Dickens, it is said, is vulgar. I do

not wholly deny it.   And where is Dickens
vulgar?   Is it where, with extraordinarily
sympathetic humour, he portrays a corner of
London poverty in Bleeding Heart Yard?   I
can see nothing vulgar here.   I feel no disposition in the author to push things out of
shape, or to make more out of the facts than
they deserve, or to narrow his point of view
for the sake of an easy stimulus to emotion.
But, perhaps, in his stories of the sufferings
and death of children, there is something
unworthy of a writer who can be so great.
Come and let us enjoy ourselves in watching
the death-bed of a child, is the impression produced upon me, as upon Mr. Lang, by the story
of little Paul.   Egotism is always vulgar, and
never more so than when displayed in crocodile
tears over sufferings which we linger upon with
delight at our own sensibility.

For sentimentalism, like the feebler forms of

fancy—the forms which lose themselves in idle detail—is not passionate, but is frigid.   A true passion will not rest in externals ; we are told, by the master of those who know, that poetry is more serious and more scientific than history. In other words, genuine feeling attends to its object ; spurious feeling attends only to itself.

Let me illustrate this connection once more from another art.   I have been told—I do not give the criticism as authoritative—that in Doré's illustrations to Dante, you will not find a single picture which reproduces a situation of the poem in true accordance with the text. And if an artist ever was a prey to gloating sentimentalism, such an artist, I suppose, was Doré.   So great, it would appear, was his haste to the indulgence of feeling that the attention never fairly fixed itself upon the matter which acted as a stimulus.

This much, then, we have learnt from the

easier case, the case of art and literature. Superficial judgment and the mere sensation of sense are connected with purely sensuous emotion, and minister to its self-indulgence, because the delightfulness of excited feeling, in those to whom such delightfulness has become an object of desire, withdraws the attention from the fuller grasp of its object, and therefore arrests the response of our personal frame to the larger and more profound of human purposes and ideas.

If now we turn to the harder case, in which many interests and prejudices and practical uncertainties combine to bewilder us, we shall find that the analysis which we have obtained will give us noteworthy results.

The growth of what has been called the sense of social compunction is, on the whole, a hopeful feature of our civilisation. I remember to have been struck, in reading Mr.

Greville's diary, with the effect of genuine surprise and dawning interest produced upon his mind by facts concerning the life of the poor which came to light when the cholera was at Sunderland. "We who float on the surface of society," he wrote (or to this effect), "do not, I suppose, realize what is the life of the poor." No decent man or woman to-day would plead guilty to such unsophisticated ignorance. So far we have gained.

Nor is sensitiveness of feeling on these matters to be deprecated.

The readiness and depth of the response to ideas and experiences of the life of others, in so far as they depend on the fine and ample stringing of the personal frame, mark an advance in social unity. Of sentiment, in the meaning above defined—of the direct emotional response to ideas single-heartedly attended to—the world can never have too much. It is a remarkable fact, and one which I do not think can be disputed, that a genuine sensitiveness to social needs has been found in a considerable number of prominent examples to accompany a genuine sensitiveness to poetic and pictorial beauty. The difference which I have been attempting to point out between sentiment and sentimentalism is concerned, not with the degree of emotion, but with its kind and its direction.

For, undoubtedly, with the growth of social compunction a new danger is created. The same delight in feeling for feeling's sake, which runs riot in the vulgar picture and romance, has opened to it a new and fertile field in the no longer short and simple annals of the poor. In isolated patches of hasty observation, in the uncriticised rumours and idle generalisations of the press and of common talk, we have the modern counterpart of that world of " I think," and " I feel," and " it seems to me," which Plato identified with the atmosphere of egotism and obscurantism. Does our emotion, we should ask ourselves, weld our attention closer and ever closer to the complicated phenomena of the actual life around us? Does it inspire us at once with humility and with resolution?— with the humility to be always learning and to put away childish self-opinion, and with the resolution to press, so far as our intelligence permits, into the heart and depth of the matter, caring for nothing but what is true and useful, and reckless of clamour, whether from the classes or from the masses? The votary of Science is accused of the very fault against which he struggles. Absolute humility may always be regarded as absolute pride; the thorough submission to reason necessarily involves the thorough defiance of unreason. " Reason," it is said; but what about feeling ? I reply that I have tried to show how right feeling is reasonable, and that in this reasonableness its rightness consists, and that no one can claim to have genuine feeling which is not the direct echo of apprehended truth.

The paradoxes of social causation are known in some degree to all who have social interests. And it does not appear to me that this is the time or place for specific controversy. All I desire to attempt to-day is to impress and to impress again on the few who will consent to take advice, that whereas all causation has paradoxes for the novice, the paradoxes of social causation are singularly startling. The meeting of extremes in the world of social reform is more astounding than any dissolving views. How quickly the philanthropist is transformed into the sweater and unjust competitor with regular labour, the charitable person into the dangerous foe of Trades' Unions and " Friendly Societies," the provider of food and shelter into the author of starvation and homelessness. On more controverted questions, such as the proper treatment of the very various classes known as the unemployed, it seems inappropriate to express a merely passing opinion. I will only entreat that, in all matters of this kind, we should struggle against becoming victims of the senses, and should force ourselves to attend, not only to the momentary fact of perception, but to the history and conditions which determine the permanent effect of our action, and should remember that, so far from being hard-hearted in giving such attention, we are thus following in the track of true emotion, while in being carried away by the first impression of unreasoned pity we are indulging ourselves, and showing an utter and frigid hard-heartedness to human welfare.

There is one very curious fact which I desire

to pause upon in this connection. Many of us suppose that, when we have got into statistics, we have got away from cheap fancy and indolent sentimentalism. Never was any opinion more delusive. The arithmetical fancy, the passion for calculation and results, is one of the commonest forms of a superficial imagination, and exercises a mysterious influence over half-educated minds. The temptation to calculate rather than to analyse—to fly at once to a mechanical process rather than pause for one which is laborious and demands original research, is active in many of the sciences, and within the limits of working hypothesis, it may have results of a certain very restricted value. But, in dealing with facts as facts, it is simply fatal. In Lanfrey's life of Napoleon I., the delusive power of this monomania, as it often comes to be, is very strikingly illustrated. Napoleon came more and more to be fascinated by his perfectly lucid and consistent calculations from data unreal or imperfect. Thus, such a disaster as that of the Russian campaign was aggravated by his partial precision. In a mechanical sense his preparations were adequate, and thus there was all the greater loss when the inevitable disaster overwhelmed them. I presume that this characteristic of so powerful an intellect is a profound illustration of the vicious influence of sentimentalism. Wrapped up in self-conceit and indulging in pleasurable dreams of boundless conquest, Napoleon gradually lost touch with actualities, and his calculative faculty became more and more divorced from any basis of fact.

The pages of the late Professor de Morgan are full of examples that show how readily the handling of figures becomes the organ of the crudest superstition.

The general principle which governs all

argument by calculation is this,—that figures, being only very mutilated abbreviations of fact, are wholly unsignificant, except to those who by concrete experience know precisely and completely for what facts they stand.

I found it impossible to persuade an energetic Charity Organisation Secretary in America, that you could not, as a matter of mere office-routine, tabulate the causes of distress in all cases brought before you. That a very experienced person who has handled the cases, may profitably record a judgment of their predominant causes is true. But the judgment of an outside observer is absolutely worthless ; and the best opinion loses its value when not interpreted by the same knowledge which produced it.

First to get behind the figures and see what is needed to picture the whole situation, then to get all the figures essential to complete the portrayal, is the obvious rule in dealing with statistics. What, for example, do the starvation figures for London represent? Verdicts from coroners' juries. Does—to insist on a simple condition only—does the Coroner's personality make any difference? Between 1873 and 1874, in the same district, with a change of coroner, there is a fall from 43 infant cases to none at all. This is at least noteworthy. Further, it is very sad that 31 deaths should have taken place which could be ascribed to starvation in London, in 1890, but if we observe that 20 years ago there were 100,[1] then, if we trust the figures at all, our feeling must be somewhat modified.

I have disdained to lay stress on the too numerous examples of philanthropy in which

[1] See returns from 1871 to 1890 inclusive in Mr. Loch's paper, " Returns as an instrument in Social Science." *Charity Organisation Review*, September, 1892.

sentimentalism must be pronounced insincere, being conjoined with grave irregularities of method, sometimes amounting to imposture. Yet it would be an omission not to observe that in the strictest moral sense the sentimentalist is always an impostor, because he himself, and not his ostensible object, is always the centre of his feelings. The frauds of sentimentalism are simply the climax of a mental state which is fraudulent through and through. I quote, with the comments of a skilled critic, an example in which one of the most mischievous forms of charity is appropriately recommended by a number of silly and vulgar attractions, culminating in the offer of an advertisement among the aristocracy in return for a donation of certain wares "for so good an object."

[1] " A grand bazaar is to be held in Kensington Town Hall this month in aid of the funds for the Children's Free

[1] *Charity Organisation Review*, December, 1892.

Breakfasts and the Winter Dinners for the Poor.   The list of patronesses has the appearance of a slightly abbreviated peerage.   'The stalls will represent a charming winter scene of Old London at Yuletide.   There will be many attractive novelties, and all performances on the stage in Large Hall will be FREE.'   The lady who organises the entertainment addresses letters to ladies and gentlemen with whom she has no personal acquaintance, inviting them to purchase tickets.   The inducements held out are 'the immediate patronage of H.R.H. the Princess Christian,' the pleasure of providing free meals and Christmas dinners to very poor children, and 'attractive novelties.'   In one corner of the prospectus is a woodcut representing a sick and half-clad child at an open attic window, with the legend, 'It is for such as these we plead'; in the opposite corner is a picture of a ragged urchin putting himself outside a hunk of bread and a mug of cocoa or soup.   It is a very crude appeal to benevolent impulse and some less worthy motives.   But the lady organiser varies her temptation.   The following letter (we omit names) was received by a wine merchant :—

DEAR SIR,—As I know how kind and charitable you are, I venture to ask you to be so very good as to send us a small donation of your wines for the bazaar, of which I enclose circular and complimentary tickets, and, being for so good an object as the Children's Free Breakfasts and the Winter Dinners for the Poor, I feel certain you will help us if you possibly can.   Any show-cards you may entrust me with shall have prominent places on the refreshment counter, and the attention of our patronesses shall be drawn to the excellence of your wines.   Any contribution, no matter how small, will be most gratefully acknowledged by——. Trusting you will not refuse your generous aid for so good a charity,   I remain,

&c., &c.

Charity seeketh not her own?   Well, well! was it not the same Apostle who pointed out the wisdom of being all things to all men?"

To point the contrast between the feeling of the worker and of the sentimentalist, I adduce the following comment on the above.   All who know anything of true work for the poor respect the writer's name.

"*To the Editor of the 'Charity Organisation Review.'*

"SIR,—In describing the arrangements for a charity festival last month, it may be thought that the letter you give as addressed to a wine-merchant is a solitary and extreme specimen, as indeed one might hope.

" I should like to say that such appeals form a part of the regular tactics employed in these 'charitable' transactions. Not long ago I received from the agent of one of the largest and best known firms for the sale of a particular article of food, a packet containing at least one hundred similar appeals for a gratuitous supply of this article for bazaars, with the similar bribe of displaying advertisements of it. They came from all denominations—Church, Roman Catholic, and Dissenting. These specimens were, I was told, a *small* sample of the number being continually received.

"Hardly ever have I felt such indignation as in the perusal of these documents.

"It is difficult to restrain one's temper, and one's pen in contemplating the depths into which 'charitable' England has fallen in these latter days of the nineteenth century!

"Yours faithfully,

"LOUISA TWINING."

No one can feel more strongly than I do the weak points of a criticism that is not perfectly definite in its application. Why, it may be said, if the man means anything, he means that every one is a sentimentalist who does not agree with him upon social questions. Well, I have tried, partly by the example of fine art, to point out a more objective distinction than this between the right and the wrong in feeling. It is, I admit, a distinction of tendency, but I am convinced that it will repay reflection. I am convinced that it is possible to arrest the attention, and divert it from feeling to fact, when we observe that our excitement is beginning to interest us, and that we are getting impatient of analysis and eager for results. I am convinced that it is well to preserve always a proportion between literary and practical impressions, and between statistical knowledge and the mastery of problems in the concrete. No one who has any knowledge at all, whether workman, labour-leader, or economist, will dispute to-day the obvious and admitted fact that charity is the chief factor in producing the miserable class of vagrants in England and Scotland; and many think that the interference of sentimental philanthropy, through bounty-fed industries, with the course of trade and wages, is a matter that now demands the closest attention of society. To avoid sentimentalism it is not intellectual ability that is primarily needed, nor a particular set of doctrines, nor, necessarily, very ample experience. It is the preference of thoroughness to quantity in work, and that genuineness of spirit which subordinates its feelings to their object.

I think that considerations of this kind deserve to be meditated by us who take an interest in the Ethical movement. If we will throw our influence into the scale *against* the self-indulgence of emotion and the illusions of piece-meal perception, and *for* self-suppression in face of the object, and a thorough coherent view of the life that we have occasion to apprehend, we may deserve well of our century. But if we will not make this vigorous effort on a question of simple right and wrong, what do we more than others ?

VIII.

TRAINING IN ENJOYMENT.[1]

THERE are two widespread views of enjoyment which seem far apart, but which, while from each of them we may learn something, have in common a grave defect.

We may call them the indolent view and the ascetic view. Commonplace people generally take the indolent view, though it does not on the whole represent even their practice. For them, as they think, enjoyment and recreation chiefly mean freedom from compulsory toil— amusement, entertainment. This freedom from

---

[1] Delivered at the Maria Grey Training College.

actuality forms no doubt a great part of our pleasure in the average theatre or the average novel. We are all inclined to this at times; we enjoy the sense of relaxation, the consciousness of not being bound, not being responsible; so at the theatre, where some one else has charge of amusing us, we only have to look on and criticise. Variety of perceptions and emotions on the stage brings this independence of ours home to us—in such moods everything is a sort of scene or comedy for our entertainment. This is one great root of the delight of going abroad—we like to put the sea between us and our work. For this indolent disposition at least, enjoyment is, in short, the feeling of being at play, and not at work. The fault or defect of this attitude is that it puts enjoyment rather low down in life, and makes it unworthy of much attention or of high energy. This failing reacts upon enjoyment and makes

it more and more trivial till, perhaps, it becomes vulgar.   It is a mood weak in itself,
and is strengthened in the wrong way in the
line of self-indulgence, and may even become
altogether immoral.   And we soon experience
how feeble this mood is, because after the
first few hours or days of mere relaxation our
nature cries out for something to do; and
English men and women often find some pretty
hard work to throw themselves into for fun.
As the foreigner says, we take our pleasure
"sadly."   This may have two meanings—
"emptily and pointlessly," like a dull man at
the seaside, or again, "severely and energeti-
cally," like a cricketer or mountaineer.   In the
latter sense we have no cause to be ashamed
of it.

Now the ascetic or Puritan view of enjoyment ought, one might have hoped, to be the
very opposite of the indolent view.   If life is a

strenuous career, governed by moral or religious ends, one would hope that enjoyment
also might be looked upon as something strenuous and worthy.   But the one-sidedness of the
Puritan spirit prevents that, and so the result
comes to be that enjoyment is again put quite
low down in life.   We all sympathise, to a
certain degree, in this view; we feel that idleness is a sin, perhaps *the* sin.   The idea that
you only work in order to get leisure does not
seem true to fact, unless leisure means for us,
as it did for the Greek citizen, a higher order
of work.   If enjoyment has nothing serious or
important about it, we are inclined to agree
with the Puritan that it is a contemptible thing.
But then we are met by the same difficulty as
before.   Give a dog a bad name and hang
him.   Put enjoyment low down in life, and it
will be low.   As Matthew Arnold was always
urging, the result of our Puritan training is not

elevation but sheer barbarism, at least in our enjoyments. There must be leisure and re-action, and times of freedom when we are thrown on our own resources, and if we are not interesting to ourselves in any other way, we naturally take to—what shall I say?—well, to steady drinking. The legislation of this country appears still to favour this conception of duty and enjoyment. On the one free day of the week, we are invited either to church or to the public-house; duty or religion is provided on the one hand, and enjoyment on the other. This system of ours no doubt im-presses itself on the minds of our people. A people is always educated by its laws, and our law impresses this choice upon our working population from its earliest years; there are, broadly speaking, just these alternatives for the day of freedom, and no other. They are not absolute alternatives, of course; care is taken that it may be possible to combine duty and enjoyment—the church and the public-house—within the limits of our free day. But they remain, with all reservations, the two well-marked extremes of the English people's life, outside actual bread-winning.

Now we have, perhaps, learnt something from the indolent and the ascetic notions of enjoyment, something from each separately and from both together.

(I.) The indolent person shows us that it is not enjoyment if it is not free, if the mind is not at play in it.

(II.) The Puritan shows us that enjoyment is contemptible if it is incapable of entering into a serious plan of life.

(III.) But we see from both together that if enjoyment is treated as trivial, then trivial, or worse, it will be.

Now, in the first place, it ought to strike

us, as against the idea that enjoyment must be trivial, that enjoyment is not wholly opposed to work. Many people, perhaps most healthy people, really delight in their work when they are once set down to it, although there is often a degree of reluctance to begin, to get into harness. This means that although our daily task is necessary to be done, we have got an interest in it that makes us feel it free or voluntary, as soon as we can forget that it is in truth compulsory. That is the fact, and so many good men now are telling us that every one ought to have work which he can enjoy or feel free in. And this is very desirable, but yet there will be always a good deal of mechanical and distasteful drudgery, which somebody must do; and all regular compulsory work is liable to be distasteful at times for reasons of health or overpressure or ill-success. And it is not desirable, even if possible, to make people really free from their work, free to leave off whenever it gets heavy and begins to drag a little. If we made ourselves thus "free," we should destroy the masculine temper of the mind, and indeed no resolute person would consent to be relieved from his duty whenever it became troublesome. So, while work should be as interesting as possible, and may be very enjoyable indeed, it will always, if only by our own undertaking, be compulsory as well as free, and may be of a kind that cannot by itself satisfy a human intelligence.

So that the solution is not to be found altogether in taking interest in our work, although that may, in various degrees, fulfil the conditions of true enjoyment. There is something else to be considered.

We saw that play, or sport, or relaxation, is not always indolent, but may be very severe and energetic. In climbing up a Scotch mountain under a burning sun, one may have wondered "why do we go through this frightful toil, no man compelling us?" But, of course, we know that the whole day would not be such good fun unless we took it as it comes. The only thing that makes it sport or play is, that underneath it all, however severe the day's work may be, there is the feeling of freedom; it is a discharge of superfluous energy; it is my own choice : there is no purpose that binds me to do it, no object, except the exertion and experience itself—it is, as we may say, disinterested. It is not even a duty, except in the general sense, that there is a duty to use one's time to good purpose. However serious, then, or energetic the sport may be, so long as it is chosen for its own sake, we are still at play, unless we make sport into a profession, which seems to me always to be an unfortunate thing, and to destroy its existence *as* sport.

Play, then, may be as serious and difficult in its nature as we like. We feel free in it, as the indolent man demands, but not because it is easy, rather because it is disinterested ; that is to say, not merely disinterested as being free from a selfish motive, but disinterested as having no motive beyond the pleasure of what we are doing and perceiving. Sensuous pleasure by itself is not true play; it has not the sense of pure freedom and self-expression.

It follows from this that there may be quite as difficult a training to go through for play as for work. In fact (to quote Mr. Pater [1] on Lacedæmon) " the surprise of St. Paul, as a practical man, at the slightness of the reward for which a Greek spent himself, natural as it is about all pagan perfection, is especially ap-plicable about these Lacedæmonians, who in-deed had actually invented that so 'corruptible'

---

[1] " Plato and Platonism," p. 212.

and essentially worthless parsley crown in place of the more tangible prizes of an earlier age."

This, however, again introduces the element of competition, which does not belong to play pure and simple, and is quite incompatible with the higher forms of it, being an interest outside the enjoyment of the play itself. But the feeling of the Greek was not merely for victory over another, but for the perfectness of the self-expression and self-mastery which that success only sealed and guaranteed. As we all know, the word which to the Greek meant "leisure" has become our word "school"—so disinterested was their devotion to those studies which for us are associated with compulsion.

Hard work, however, is happily no great deterrent to the English mind. To excel in cricket or in rowing there is no labour that an English lad will shirk, though he expects nothing from these arts, except, quite in a Platonic spirit, their own highest perfection. We may then suppose, I think, at this point that it is not laziness or self-indulgence, but in the sense which has been explained, disinterestedness and self-expression, or freedom and spontaneity, which really distinguish enjoyment from work.

If this is so, it seems to follow that study and discipline are not incompatible with enjoyment, and that quite possibly it may be true, as the old Greeks have told us, and as the Puritan contention has suggested though not accepted, that the beautiful or noble is difficult. Great philosophers have explained how man is most truly at play, most disinterested, most spontaneous, endowed with the deepest self-expression, when he enjoys what is beautiful, or pours out his soul in art.

The power of enjoyment, then, in the truest

and fullest sense, needs, like other capacities, to be developed by training. It does not come of itself, and even the most careful education can only put the instruments in our hands and cannot endow us with the persistency and goodwill to use them. We may easily—how easily!—by sloth or carelessness in our formative years, leave uncultivated whole provinces of our nature which we shall wish to harvest when it is too late. A dreary misconception on this matter has been represented, I fear unconsciously, by a clever novelist of our own day. The story is that a woman, not without capacity, when her little world of passion is falling to pieces, hits upon the fancy that study and culture may possibly be a consolation to her. But seeking rest and comfort in intellectual labour, she can find none; and, so it seems to be implied, the interests of the intelligence are therefore shown to be a pale and empty mockery. But the true moral is different. It is, that the great interests of life will not come to one by magic, at a single call, as an amusement to the vacant mind; for all, except unusually gifted natures, it is necessary to worship the Muses early and resolutely, if we desire to enjoy their gifts at our utmost need.

There are two necessities to be kept in view if we would avoid the most dangerous absurdities. The first is the necessity of discipline; the second is the necessity of enjoyment. I will say a few words about each.

The necessity of discipline for the learner corresponds to the necessity of selection for the artist. We have a natural attentiveness, a natural inclination to throw our interests into the things around us. But our world is to begin with a confusion of objects and ideas, and our attention is readily caught, readily bewildered, and, when bewildered, readily fatigued. The work of art operates by selection—and the more brilliant and complicated it is, the selection by which it exists is so much the more severely appropriate and coherent. For the essence of beauty is expression, and expression depends on intelligent connection. Therefore, to the immature attention, the higher forms of beauty are too severe, or too intricate for enjoyment. Instead of playing over a surface of scattered forms or ideas, the attention is by them called upon to follow a clue which has, so to speak, a logical character. The distractions in which it delights are pruned away; nothing is there but what bears upon the central thought, and carries the stamp of the governing emotion. Why, this, it may be said, is to simplify, to make easy, not to make hard; such beauty must surely be easier to the attention than

the confused scenery of every day! Well,
here is the paradox; a restrained and reserved
beauty is easy in a sense; but only to an
attention which is concentrated on a single
idea. Now it is an effort to concentrate
attention, and to pursue a single idea. Our
ordinary consciousness is a succession of distractions. In a similar sense, it might be said,
the theory of gravitation is "simpler" than
our perception of the falling rain.

Experience bears this out. In the training
of the average individual learner, or in the
reawakening of degraded ages, the art of a
decadence is appreciated sooner than that
which bears the classical stamp. And this is
equally true, whether the classic in question
be simple or intricate. It is hard because of
its purity, and in this sense Shakespeare is as
hard as Sophocles. It is a strange but instructive example to read the proceedings of

the Committee which was appointed by the English Government, in 1815, to discuss the proposed purchase of the Elgin marbles. The report is probably familiar to some of you, through the lecture by Miss Sellers, which was published in the *Univ. Ext. Journal.* Flaxman, you may remember, preferred the Apollo Belvedere to the Theseus of the Parthenon. A connoisseur was found to testify that the Theseus was spurious, and "the rest of the articles very poor." I think we can understand how this comes about. The overblown or superfluous attraction of decadent art catches the attention of the man in the street more readily than the pure outline which is severely faithful to its idea. But, how—you may ask—can the modern poet or artist be in this sense classical? In Shakespeare, for example, we surely have humour and romance, fascination of every hue and texture, and restraint or reserve has here no place nor meaning. But it is not exactly so. Shakespeare, like all great artists, has his severity. He has the severity, and the logic of Nature. He terrifies the effeminate, shocks the conventional, and over-burdens the weak. Let me read the confession of a great mind strong enough to be candid. It is Schiller who writes: "When at an early age I first became acquainted with Shakespeare, I was indignant at his coldness, his insensibility, which permitted him to jest in the moments of highest emotion, to let the clown break in upon the most heart-rending scenes of *Hamlet, Lear, Macbeth.* . . . Misled by my acquaintance with recent poetry so as in every work to look first for the poet, to meet him heart to heart, I found it intolerable that here the poet never showed himself, and would not let me question him. I was not yet capable of understanding nature at first hand. I could only endure the picture of it as reflected through the understanding, and to that end the French sentimental poets and the 18th century Germans were the right people for me." However various Shakespeare may be, he is always coherent, and however natural, he calls upon us to follow him beyond our everyday selves.

Simply, then, to follow the great masters in any art, or to see nature in their spirit, a serious discipline of attention is presupposed. Only that beauty will afford the more permanent and energetic enjoyment which in return for its great expressiveness—I am borrowing Mr. Pater's phrases—demands from us a great attentiveness. It is idle to consult the oracles of the newspaper press for the best one hundred books; from such prescriptions as theirs, we shall gain no true guidance, we shall acquire no new capacity for organising our attention and our likings. We all know enough to make a beginning in the direction which our capacities may point out; it is want of energy, and a prejudice that enjoyment ought not to be laborious, which generally stands in our way. Every one indeed has not every talent, and prudence suggests that after fair trial we should abandon the paths in which we feel no possibility of progress. The obstacles due to sheer incapacity—as for example, to the lack of a musical ear—must be carefully distinguished from those due to indolence; and there is no greater test of good sense than the choice of directions in which we hope our interest to develop. For this is the key to our problem—the development of definite interests, and not the mere entertainment of leisure.

An experienced educationist said to me not

long ago—and it was an instructive heresy—
"that 'harmonious development of the whole
mind' is the greatest conceivable absurdity."
What he meant was this: that the development
must not be so generally harmonious as not
to be a development at all, or, as Hegel loves
to insist, "you must become *something* if you
mean to be *anything*." A healthy boy, as a
rule, is learning chiefly one thing at one
period of his life. It is good to be mastered
by an interest, although it is good, too, to learn
balance and self-restraint. In a great degree
we must, as the artist does, proceed by selection. Giving this and that a trial, according
to our opportunities, we should yet, when we
feel our feet in any one ascent, see to it that
we climb vigorously, and spare no labour to
adapt our attention to the element for which
we feel an affinity. We should not be deterred by the idleness of our own mind, or of

others, but should, if necessary, work through, with some pains and labour, those master-pieces which the judgment of the ages has crowned. Like the prudent buyer of pictures, we should attend to what we are convinced is a little above our present capacity, though in the direction of its development, and thus break the fetters of chance and indolence. The mere greatness of a good may conceal it from the unpractised eye, just as the common-place novelist will satirise the wearisomeness of classical music; as if the ear accustomed to Offenbach was embarrassed and outwearied by the too abundant melody of Beethoven. Especially in the case of works removed from us by long intervals of history, we must expect to go through a certain preparation, whether literally or metaphorically the learning of a new language, before, as with Homer's heroes when the gods are favourable, the cloud is lifted from our eyes, and we are taught to discern the earthly from the divine. And the same is true of the great Book of Nature. Its language may be learned in many different ways, with the poet, over the sketch book, in the biological laboratory, or under the guidance of the field botanist or geologist. But in one way or another our attentiveness must match Nature's expressiveness before we shall have learned to read the intelligence that she reveals. Study, patience, humility, to attend to the object, to forget our trivial selves—these are the elements of discipline that go to a training in enjoyment.

But there is another side to the matter. Scholarship, study, the discipline of attention, are necessary things, and the very purity and vigour—the true asceticism which they involve, are elements of masculine enjoyment. After all, however, it is the most terrible of errors to take the means for the end. Enjoyment is a delusion, if we do not enjoy; and though the man in the street who condemns art-scholarship is a Philistine, yet the scholar who does not enjoy is no less assuredly a pedant. Here is the knot and paradox of the whole matter, the point whence self-deception enters in, and where we hardly know how to steer between pedantry and Philistinism. Is it enjoyment when we have to wrestle for dear life with George Meredith, or with Browning, with Dante, Æschylus, or Pindar? If we give up the task, is it indolence or genuineness? If we persevere, is it true love or pedantry? No general criterion can be laid down; of course a partial difficulty, even one artistically unpardonable, may be faced for the sake of the whole, which its solution may illuminate; but apart from this, even the strain of straightforward insight and the burden of significance may be so great that we hardly know whether we persevere as a fancied duty or as a genuine pleasure. I do not suppose that most people, if they were simply desirous to spend the pleasantest hour, would take down —say *King Lear*, from the bookshelf. The fact is, that the enjoyment of beauty in its higher form is not very adequately characterised by the term " pleasant." Enjoyment is the safer word, because it implies something more definite, perhaps more active—it suggests *enjoying ourselves.* This is what we must do, in the end, if our training in enjoyment has not been pedantry. We must feel that we are free and disinterested, laying hold upon our true selves, exalted out of our every-day routine. We may know all mysteries, and all knowledge; the secrets of archæology or of physical acoustics may lie open before us, but if we do not in the end *enjoy* ourselves

we are pretentious pedants, we are " as sound-
ing brass and a tinkling cymbal."

In conclusion, I may say a word, by way of
illustration, on one or two practical problems.
It is quite indisputable, in my opinion, that
silly occupations and sheer waste of leisure
upon trifles, destroy the higher life of many
men and women. In the case of women the
fault is not wholly their own. There is still far
too strong a tradition that a woman has no independent life, and that she exists as a social
ornament, as a plaything, or as a drudge. If a
girl, therefore, begs for a few hours in the day,
undisturbed by needless conversation or superfluous social routine, she is apt to be regarded
as unwomanly, and as averse to the true duties
of the household. For this charge I have never
observed any foundation. I am sure that the
idle woman is a far greater danger to domesti-
city than even the too eager student. And it

is hard to exaggerate the importance of a woman's education.   In every household, the general level of thought and conversation is dictated by the habits and likings of the women.   With young men there are parallel dangers to those which beset young women. I have been told by the experienced head of a great college, that while athleticism might be good enough in itself, it tended to bring with it the intolerable evil of an ever-present subject of facile and effortless conversation.

But all this being so, a degree of resolution is required to bend the mind to things which, at the outset, are less immediately amusing than personal or sporting gossip, or a commonplace game or novel.   Yet the choice remains, and is all-important for life.   With skill and resolution, leisure may be found to study the great poets of our own country and of the modern world, and also, perhaps, the great authors of ancient times, in the admirable translations now accessible. When an interest has been acquired in the life of any age, a first-rate history will be as fascinating as a romance, and all kinds of human achievement will assume a fresh significance from a study of the conditions under which they arise. Whether, for example, the Greek language should be learned, is a question demanding great individual judgment. To have mastered it, is to have the key to a literature which even our own can hardly parallel. But time is limited— strength still more so. If the period of greatest leisure is likely to be short, it is a doubtful policy to consume it all in acquiring an instrument which there may not be much time to use. Many and many men and women who grasp the Greek mind, not through the language, but through a true sense of beauty and of duty, have more sympathy with Homer or Pericles or Plato than any scholar of the purely antiquarian type. To acquire the habit of studying what demands serious effort, by way of enjoyment, is in any case, here as else-where, the essential point. It must be remembered that in the sculptures at the Museum we have the Greeks at first hand for those who have eyes to see.

One further point before I close. There is, no doubt, a risk of pedantry in a scheme of life, in fixed *hours*, so to speak, of devotion. Yet perhaps those interests which are not safe-guarded by the pressure of daily necessity, may without injury be the object of some formal attention—some season set apart, some quiet time, habitually consecrated to the study of what is great. For a somewhat different pur-pose, and to ensure that familiarity without which no work of Art can be truly loved, I have found that the gatherings called Shakespeare readings, have considerable value. It is a great thing to be taken through play after play with the thoroughness that comes of reading aloud. I would keep all such societies pretty clear of discussion and explanation. Necessary criticism should be got by each for himself from the best books; but the tendency to discussion and explanation is not very fortunate, except among highly skilled critics, and most people are better employed in becoming familiar with works of Art than in trying to explain them. One can often see, even in published papers of these societies, that they are immature fancies, which a loyal and persevering study of the work would probably have reduced to their true dimensions. Such meetings, in short, should be for pure enjoyment.

However all this may be, we cannot go wrong in studying what is great, and conquering the first difficulties of its novelty or intricacy, and of our wandering attention, while we are young and have some leisure, and our minds are energetic and flexible. Then, with fresh experience, there comes always fresh light, and we may hope in later life to grow steadily and continuously, and without severe labour, in the power of enjoying ourselves—of enjoying, that is, the human mind at its best, which will more and more become a part of our own being.

IX.

LUXURY AND REFINEMENT.[1]

THERE is a great deal to be said in favour of devoting our moral attention rather to subjects of everyday practice than to unique examples of heroism. We all agree, indeed, that a morality is unsound which omits our daily conduct, but it may be doubted whether we fully perceive either the depth and thoroughness of which commonplace duties are capable, or the hazards which attend a strained admiration for striking achievement. It might even be urged that the figure implied in our current phrases

---

[1] Delivered at Essex Hall for the London Ethical Society.

which unite elevation with the ideal is not the most fortunate that might have been chosen. If sometimes we were to think less of a "high ideal," and more, as Plato has warned us with a foresight unappreciated by his interpreters, of an intelligent, that is, a discriminating and coherent view of life—the view of one who is awake and not lost in dreams—we should be gainers morally no less than intellectually. Could we not exercise our imagination by asking ourselves at times not only whether our ideal can be called lofty, but how it would bear combination with such adjectives as deep, wide, solid, thorough, intelligent? The first meaning of "height" is naturally remoteness and the beyond, and suggests the mere star-gazing attitude which Plato condemns in the moralist as in the astronomer.

And so, in feeding the mind principally upon heroic examples, or great and successful enterprises, there is a serious hazard that the whole aim of moral nurture should be defeated, that emotion should be substituted for action, and the saint or hero, through our unconscious tendency to accept a vicarious atonement, should be regarded as carrying the burden which is really ours. I confess that much of the praise and honour lavished by an indolent but sensitive society, now upon those who deserve it, and now again upon those who deserve something different, has to my perceptions a disagreeable quality. Behind all the gratitude and satisfaction I seem to detect first a thrill of sensibility over the pathetic newspaper paragraph, or the exciting annual report, and then the complacency which congratulates itself on the splendid work that is being done by others, and so passes to the order of the day.

A subject such as that to which I invite your attention has, therefore, I venture to think, a moral importance of a peculiar and definite kind.

In the first place, the demand which it implies is humble, and therefore is a reality. No one can plead that it is above him. The circumstances and relations with which it deals are necessarily a part of every civilized life. It is therefore a universal problem. Moreover, while thus universal, it is also profound. It does not indeed lead us to require from ourselves immense self-sacrifice, or heroic enterprise. The path to which it points is in appearance easy and pleasant enough. It is marked out by the best purposes of life—purposes which rest upon the sense of life as a whole—and fenced in by daily and hourly watchfulness and self-respect. Yet, as the Greek well knew, temperance is akin to courage, and he is no mean soldier of the social army who is able to maintain through every circumstance of position and expenditure, the conviction of Plato's knightly order—that that is always to be done which tends to social well-being.

If, moreover, the requirements imposed on individual conduct by attention to this subject are more serious than might appear, so also are the social and economic bearings which in part account for such requirements. We see at once that we are dealing with nothing less than the whole problem of wants—of consumption. Here we come in contact on the one hand with the control of production, including the conditions under which it is carried on, and the kind of objects upon which labour has to be expended. On the other hand we are touching the standard of life, which is in a great degree set by one class to another, and is everywhere, and not merely among the wealthy, a modifiable conception. The effect produced unconsciously by habits of the well-to-do, which, though occasional in their own lives, are persistent in relation to those who minister to them, is strikingly elucidated by the following passage from Mr. Charles Booth's work on "Life and Labour in London," vol. ii., p. 229.

"The bright and busy life for which the hotels and theatres exist, which supports the fashionable shops, and which fills the roadways with an endless stream of carriages and cabs and the footwalks at all times of the day and far into the night with a well-dressed crowd, is altogether outside of the Central London we have been attempting to describe. Those who enjoy this life come on pleasure bent, with money in their pockets, from all parts of London, from all parts of England, and from all parts of the world. They come and they go ; and are divorced from the sense of responsibility which arises naturally from living in the reflected light of our past actions, and pursued by their consequences. Extravagance, which is the exception in the life of each individual, becomes the rule in a state of things which is the sum of these exceptions. The result is a strange world ; at best, not altogether whole-some ; at worst, inexpressibly vicious. Domestic virtues have no very definite place in it, and moral laws are too often disregarded. There results, to some extent, a malign influence upon those who live to supply the many needs of these gay wayfarers. Imposition of all kinds is passed over with a shrug for the sake of present ease. Money will be given to the dishonest beggar or bullying tout whose face the giver will never see again. Partly perhaps as a result of this influence, the population of the district differs much in character from that of East or South London, or probably that of any other part. So say those of the clergy who have experience which enables them to make the comparison. Its people are, it is said, more conscious. If they are bad, they know it ; if they are poor, they feel it more. They are clever, ingenious talkers, and if they beg are astute beggars. They are interesting enough, but from the point of view of the Church, very difficult ' to get hold of.' Perhaps they may at times have the best of an argument relied on to convince them of their errors."

And last, but not least, our relations of daily intercourse are immensely affected by the prevalent standard of refinement. The barrier between some and others is not really difference in wealth, nor antagonism of industrial interests ; it is a lack of subjects in common to talk about when we meet. Luxury intensifies the barrier, because its enjoyments are exclusive.   Refinement weakens it, because its enjoyments are universal.   A very great part at least of our class distinctions to-day have no necessary ground in material differences, and simply rest on oppositions of habit and ideas which a little care and goodwill might remove in the course of a generation.

The limits of our treatment must be narrow relatively to the subject, for it is as wide and as complex as life itself.   I do not aim at more than laying down a general principle, insisting on the importance of the matter, and claiming that attention to it should be regarded as a duty.

Let us try whether we can find a tolerable definition which will exhibit the essential contrast between Luxury and Refinement.

Both are phenomena of man's conquest over nature.   Neither the one nor the other can appear until current wants have come to be satisfied with regularity, and there is a super-fluity which can be dealt with at pleasure, either by way of self-indulgence, or as a means to larger purposes.

Luxury, then, in its most general aspect, might be taken as equivalent to man's subjugation by his own conquest of nature. Refinement, as the full opposite on the same basis, would then appear to consist in man's triumph over his own conquest of nature. I do not say that these definitions will absolutely hold, but they will serve, perhaps, as starting points for discussion.

Within each of these habits or tendencies it would seem that we may further distinguish a practical and a contemplative side.

In Luxury there may be Self-indulgence or Ostentation. In Refinement we may observe both Comfort and Beauty.

We will first consider the natural impulse,

as we may call it, taking natural to mean unperverted,—the impulse or habit of refinement—and then the form which from a moral point of view may be ranked as its corruption, that is to say, the tendency to luxury.

In refinement, then, the conquest of nature, with the resources and superfluities implied by such a conquest, has been made subservient to distinctly human ends. The conqueror is a conqueror still and has not been subjugated by his captive.

To the ordinary life in which this relation is exhibited we apply the term Comfort, which though often disparagingly used, is quite capable of an honourable meaning.

Comfort, as a form of refinement, no less than self-indulgence as a form of luxury, may be contrasted with the barely necessary. Man, as Carlyle has taught us, reaches beyond mere needs even before he has satisfied them.

His demand for self-assertion does not wholly cease at any level of misery, but may always be traced, in however wretched a form, by the side of or within the animal wants which make for bare life. It is vain to think of reducing human comfort to what is necessary for the support of existence. It may, however, be replied that necessity itself is relative, and that comfort simply means the possession of what is necessary for a more complex life, as bare sustenance means the possession of what is necessary for a merely animal life. But this is not precisely true. At every level of life comfort may be distinguished from bare suf-ficiency, and the distinction seems to be of the following kind. Comfort, no doubt, retains the outline of necessity. It is relative to the aims and therefore to the wants of man at the stage which he has reached. But in re-lation to every want it includes a margin of self-assertion.   It is, so to speak, symbolic. The degree of cleanliness, for instance, which an Englishman includes in his notion of comfort, is not viewed by him simply as essential to health, or to the durability of his possessions which slovenliness might impair. There is a conscious emphasis or self-assertion involved.   We desire not merely to be free in fact from the risk of poison, or nastiness, or the disfigurement of our beautiful things, but to set a distinct margin between us and the objectionable contact.   We are not comfortable unless the satisfaction of our needs is symbolized or accented as well as realized. So again in hospitality.   It is a cheap sneer to ask why what is good enough for me is not good enough for my guest.   I desire, and rightly desire, to betray a conscious attention, to insist, by some additional ceremony, however trifling, that I am alive to the duty imposed upon me as a host. In all these matters true comfort represents a perfectly right and desirable convention, the self-assertion of a human being which is determined not merely to have its necessities met, but to express itself in the mode and degree in which they are met. Of course, the convention may readily degenerate into pedantry, which often arises in these matters from mere want of thought. The tendency is always to push forward, and improve upon every improvement; and it is only too easy to depart altogether from the general outline prescribed by reasonable purpose or human necessity. In such a case we have passed the boundary line between refinement and luxury, because we have allowed ourselves to be enslaved by our own command over nature.

But the limit is rational, not quantitative. In many respects more comfort is desirable than any but the very wealthiest of us have attained. The mere exclusiveness of the first-class passenger by rail may be vulgar; but for hardworked women or men, making the best use of their brief holiday, it is plain that overcrowding, a cramped position, or insufficient ventilation on a long journey, are drawbacks without any moral advantage. Nor is there any merit in wasting the strength of valuable workers by knocking them to pieces in jolting cabs or omnibuses. A far higher standard than at present exists in this respect would be conducive to efficiency and good life throughout the whole of society. More and more, we may further observe, as the general standard rises, it absorbs into itself what has hitherto been the standard of exclusive classes; and the omnibus and the tramcar, and the third-class railway carriage rank among the most democratic influences of to-day. We hope, then, as comfort is rational-ised and humanised, that on the one hand the idea of what is "appropriate to your station" will disappear; but, on the other hand, the means of a reasonable way of life, how-ever costly, may become the appanage of all members of the community. Among such means, for example, I should reckon a yearly holiday in the neighbourhood of sea or moun-tain. I am not discussing how it should be provided, and am far from suggesting that any short cut to such a state of things is possible. But it does appear to me that the demarcation between comfort and self-indulgence is not primarily a question of costliness, but a question of relevancy to the aims of life. True comfort may be costly, its cost may even be prohibitive; but it is always reasonable.

The higher stage of refinement is reached

when we have so subordinated nature to ourselves, have so subjected our mastery over it to distinctively human aims, that material things become expressive of our minds and responsive to our moods. This is the creation or the perception of beauty. The great value of it is that it means vitality. Far from being languid or effeminate, it depends upon a strong life, such as leaves a mark on its surroundings. Nothing that exhibits a significance can be ugly in the worst sense.

But of beauty, too, as of comfort, it may be complained that it is costly. Costly it certainly must be in thought and affection; but expenditure of this kind enriches those who make it. No doubt, also, the greater works of beauty, being the rare productions of high capacity and devotion, will, as a rule, be costly in the terms of commercial exchange. But yet the complaint, if stated as an objection to our demand, is altogether misconceived. The simple but careful regard for what is best in life, which accompanies a true devotedness to the beautiful, can make itself felt within the narrowest means and tends to plain and methodical management. The careless or ill-balanced temper which permits or indulges in commonplace ornament or pretentious ugliness, tends to be accompanied by folly and extravagance, for it has no conception of life as a whole. Just as it is the thrifty house-wife who can show the best clothed and best nourished family, so the mind that is en-thusiastic in the cause of beauty will be that which is endowed with self-restraint and unity of purpose to control expenditure most effici-ently. In fact, as we see every day, ugliness is not at its worst where resources are narrowest. How exquisitely the simple room is lit up by the single vase of flowers, or the classical photograph, or the little shelf of first-rate books.

We are not now dealing with the specific question of æsthetic training, but only with the general attitude of mind which distinguishes refinement from luxury. And we find this attitude in the care for unity and organisation, determined by distinctively human aims throughout our external surroundings, whether with a view to the self-respecting satisfaction in the meeting of our every-day wants and purposes which we call comfort, or with a view to the expression of our deeper selves in the order and selection of our visible world, which we call beauty. I urge that attention to these matters is a duty, and that it ought to be also a pleasure ; yet in the continuous demand for definite purpose, and for strength of self-mastery, to the exclusion of chance desires, and of flaccid and fluid living, it will lay upon us a stronger moral grasp than we anticipate, while its social results will be of quite incalculable importance.

Luxury, we thought, is the full opposite of refinement, on the same basis. We fall into it when we become slaves of our own conquest of nature, so that means become ends to us. The whole question, in fact, is a problem of the right relation between means and ends.

When we are enslaved through the pursuit of private pleasure, we are in the primary phase of luxury, to which we gave the name of self-indulgence. It does not appear that any measure, any sumptuary rule, can be taken to distinguish the self-indulgence of luxury from the comfort of refinement. The question must always turn on relevancy to distinctively human aims. When the non-human element is uppermost, permeated as it always is in man by the moral self craving for satisfaction which that element cannot afford it, then we have self-indulgence. The means have become the end. Here of course, an infinity of self-deception is possible. We are not attempting to lay down practical rules, but merely to suggest clues for *bonâ fide* enquirers.

There is one great group of dangers to-day by which the nature of the problem may be illustrated. Traditions and class sentiments are breaking down. The choice is thrown more and more on the individual. Simplicity and directness are coming into vogue, as opposed to ceremony and formalism. Now simplicity may mean many things. Among others, it may very well mean the departure from a rule which involved some self-respect and some self-denial. Thackeray has taught us to laugh at the stingy aristocrat whose silver side-dishes had very little food upon them. Trollope has preached to us to care for the substantials of hospitality, and not sacrifice them to display. In the cases depicted we are carried away by the satirist. Yet is it so plain that eating and drinking are greater goods than respect for the ornaments of an ancient house, or that the tradition of austerity, which was an element of the ways of our fathers, in the home, in the school, and in the college, ought to be wholly flung aside under the pretext of going straight to the essentials of life? We must look to it that our revolt against ceremony shall not mean the victory of the lower over the higher senses, of the animal appetites over the sense of form. The individual to-day has to shape his own life. Self-indulgence—the inversion of means and ends—arises by a natural progression. Invention, improvement, ingenuity, are pleasurable in themselves. One means of satisfaction suggests another; we grow interested, and push the matter further, till the merest means of living have become a grotesque and gigantic tyranny, and the human purpose which they were to subserve has altogether escaped from the mind. The man, as we say, has *forgotten himself.*

The expression of hospitality in all its forms is a case in point. It may be overweighted by its own machinery, and this without any special iniquity on the part of those responsible, but simply because of the omission to control the automatic increase of the means of indulgence and commonplace entertainment by a habitual reference to what is really worth having and doing. There is no panacea for these evils. Nothing will remedy them but an effectual attention to the idea of life as a whole and a consideration whether its best purposes are being helped or hindered by our arrangements.

When, on the other hand, we are enslaved

by the nature we have subjugated, or by the fact of its subjection to us, in relation to our vanity, we may be said to fall into Ostentation.

It is worth while to observe at once that Ostentation, no less than self-indulgence, is fatal to beauty. No form of luxury, as here defined, is compatible with æsthetic enjoyment. Luxury involves the thought of our private satisfaction ; refinement, in both its forms, the thought of our satisfaction in ideas or purposes greater than our sensuous selves. When we are craving for beauty we cannot, in the ordinary sense of the words, be thinking about ourselves. We shall be entering into the significance of things, and not attending to our own feelings of gratification. But if we have not enough wit or unselfishness to lose ourselves in anything interesting, then our surroundings will be distorted by the reflection of our vulgarity. True expressiveness will be replaced by repetition, size, or costliness. Wishing to impress ourselves on others, we shall impress upon our external life this wish and no more.

The fault is incurred readily and sometimes all but unconsciously.   Our circumstances or the action of others urge us to "forget" our "truer selves."   How beautiful and significant, for example, is the custom of strewing flowers on the last resting-place of those who are dear to us :

> "Strew on her roses, roses,
>   And never a spray of yew."

But if this natural tribute assume the dimensions of a mechanical output furnished by a society that has lost the sense of measure, so that masses of vegetable matter pour in from the florist, taxing the patience of those who have much else to think of than undertaking the work of decorators, here it may reasonably be thought that the means have become an excrescence which is a positive hindrance to the end.

The question of Fashion is far from simple. I incline to treat the fashions as a caricature of something which is really necessary. There seem to be good reasons both for a prevailing custom and for frequent change in dress and in decoration. New needs arise, such as more athletic habits and outdoor life. New inventions, like the electric light, make new demands on the decorative instinct; or a powerful genius, seconding a deep-seated change in the world of taste, forces on the popular mind fresh beauties of colour and design. Now in all these matters most people must imitate. We cannot all be originators; to adopt what is good, when offered to us, is as much as most of us can hope. Nor should originality be confounded with eccentricity. I have heard of people who were so afraid of compromising their originality by yielding to the influence of a great genius, that they threw themselves into the arms of his second-rate imitators.

Then, if there is to be change, there must be some tyranny. New things must in some degree drive out old; a shop cannot keep, nor a factory produce, all the stuffs that have ever been made. It is denied that Greek women had fashions in dress. I should be much surprised if they had not; but if they had not, it was probably because women had no independent life. We certainly hear of changes that are analogous to change of fashion in the costumes of Athenian men. Theoretically speaking, one would be inclined to suggest that the mere change of minds and habits, inevitable in a progressive society, must bring with it novelties in costume and decoration.

But though this be true, it is still possible

that fashion as it exists may be a caricature of the real need—may be related to it as Ostentation to the sense of Beauty.   It seems to be doubtful whether the modes of women's dress are on the whole progressive in respect of taste, or healthiness, or convenience.   It is alleged that fashion is needlessly tyrannical, *i.e.* causes waste by marked changes at short intervals, suggestive of the desire to outstrip others in a race of ostentation.   A careful study of this matter, considering its very important social bearings, would be well worth undertaking by some competent woman.

In conclusion, we must recur for a moment to a difficulty which is sure to arise in many minds to-day.   It is that on which we said a few words in treating of Refinement.   How far, it will be asked, is the due organisation of external life according to its higher purposes hindered by sheer poverty?   To begin with, we may lay it down generally that the disposition to such organisation, and the reverse, shows itself far below the lowest level which we should recognise as that of comfortable sustenance. It is in fact an element of humanity, and asserts itself as soon as any human qualities assert themselves. Order, cleanliness, personal neatness, are marks as distinctive of character in the homes of unskilled labourers as in the houses of the middle class. To approach the matter more in detail, we should bear in mind that the one universal rule of scientific method is to " break up the problem." This is what we cannot persuade the commonplace writers on such matters to attempt. Society is composed, not of "the poor" and "the rich," but of an immense variety of economic classes, all in contact along their margins, and all, but principally those immediately contiguous, influencing each other.

That it is not poverty which mainly hinders improvement is plain from the fact that the evils which cause improvement to be demanded, can exist in their acutest form only where improvement is materially possible, and do exist in this form in full one-half of society. Progress is impossible unless those for whom it is easiest will lead the way; and by the time that they—one-half at least of the community, for I definitely include the well-to-do mechanics —have made a positive advance, the position of those below them, and their capacities, will have been profoundly modified by the influence of this advance itself.   It is sometimes implied that individual efforts are of no use, and individual phenomena of no significance.   But this is as false as false can be.   All individual change may be thought isolated; but none of it can be so in truth.   The transformation of an individual mind is a change in the atmosphere of all surrounding minds; and the change of mental atmosphere is the most significant of changes. It is needless at this time of day to enumerate examples, though I have any number at hand, in order to demonstrate the possibilities of life among English peasants and mechanics.[1] Nor would my argument be unimportant in its range, if applied to our enormous middle class alone. I will rather sustain the reality of the problem from the other side, by showing how much has been developed to meet the ordinary needs and views of our prosperous working class, which clearly exhibits at once the need of a change, and the resources which make it possible.

---

[1] One, however, a small library started and maintained by a knot of London workmen, and managed by their own committee, though with outside assistance and advice, and with a small guarantee for expenses, which has never been fully drawn on, is to me of peculiar interest.

The following extract is from a letter describing one of those seaside resorts which receive crowds of mechanics with their families for a short time in the summer months. It carries its own moral.

" M. is clearly the resort of mechanics, shopfolk and the like,—' markets' are not food, but china and toy shops. Miles of awful jugs and cups ' A present from M.'—of M. rock—a dreadful red and yellow sweet, and M. pebbles —*i.e.* common beach stones at one penny per lb. There's a ' People's Palace,' ten hours entertainment for sixpence, and a comic singer and band twice a day on the Pier—at the Pier end are one or two covered sitting places, grim and hideous and dirty—one of them full of ' penny in the slot' models, that work, ' disclose the future,' etc. Said I to the keeper of a cup and jug shop, ' Are those the hills about K.?' She gazed vaguely, but a bright girl behind her

said, 'Yes,' and began to point out places—
Board School, thought I—'And what is that
smoky town?' Said the woman, 'You can't see
no smoky town from here'; 'Yes, you can—
over there.'   'I think it's W.,' said the girl;
'well now, I never noticed that before.'   The
smoke and chimneys were staring her in the
face!   The girl, obviously wide awake and
quick, had as obviously never used a tooth-
brush.   The people strike me as delightfully
independent, what a Tory would call rude.
.   .   .   Great efforts of taste in this house—
which is far above what such houses used to be
—woodwork and bedroom furniture all painted
to match, in Morrisian style; colouring not
bad, lots of fir-cone frames and so on, but one
good photograph of a Gainsborough among the
trash; and with all this not a bath, or anything
approaching one, in the house.   All sorts of
baths in the People's Palace, and I'm going to

investigate and see if they are popular. Yesterday I went out to explore, and wanted to buy a cup of tea—the whole sea front is full of eating places, but I walked nearly a mile before I found one that looked possible—*i.e.* clean, and with clean-looking cakes. I did at last discover one, and as I sat there the stream of people coming in never ceased. We are an unenterprising race; we *like* things nice, but we don't bestir ourselves to get them. It seems to me all this is typical—one sees the *amusements* and habits of people who don't look at all poor in the ordinary sense, and must have some leisure or they would not be here. . . . The sea front was full of people, men as well as families—many coming and going with hand-bags—all quite tidily, and many very comfortably, dressed. But where is the refinement in the comfort ?"

The sum and substance of the whole matter

is the importance of making it a duty to adapt our surroundings to the highest aims of life. For, among other reasons, this is the only sure basis of fellowship. I conclude with a passage which states, better than any other known to me, the ultimate bearing of the refinement which we desire. It is the final paragraph of the late Professor Green's address at the opening of the Oxford High School.[1]

"Our High School then may fairly claim to be helping forward the time when every Oxford citizen will have open to him at least the precious companionship of the best books in his own language, and the knowledge necessary to make him really independent ; when all who have a special taste for learning will have open to them what has hitherto been unpleasantly called the ' education of gentlemen.'

---

[1] T. H. Green. "Works," III. p. 475.

I confess to hoping for a time when that phrase will have lost its meaning, because the sort of education which alone makes the gentleman in any true sense will be within the reach of all. As it was the aspiration of Moses that all the Lord's people should be prophets, so with all seriousness and reverence we may hope and pray for a condition of English society in which all honest citizens will recognise themselves and be recognised by each other as gentlemen."

X.

THE ANTITHESIS BETWEEN INDIVIDUAL-
ISM AND SOCIALISM PHILOSOPHICALLY
CONSIDERED.[1]

THE purpose which I have set before myself
this evening is a very humble and limited
one. I have not come here to instruct skilled
economists and statisticians in political economy
and the use of statistics ; I have not come here
to attempt an analysis of the probable working
of Economic Socialism. I am not going to
deny, so far as I am aware, any of the fundamental principles which are really involved in
the Socialist contention. What I want to be

---

[1] A Paper read by invitation at a meeting of the Fabian
Society on February 21, 1890.

allowed to attempt is simply to state a question, to emphasise a distinction. And the good which I should hope to effect, if I had the power to effect it, would be to help in re-focussing the Socialist picture of social phenomena, not obliterating its details, but perhaps taking in a little more at both sides, and altering the light and shade, and putting some things in the foreground that are now in the background, and *vice versâ*. Or, to change the metaphor, the Socialist express seems to me to be at present approaching a junction. I do not want it to shut off steam, but I wish I could be pointsman when it comes up; for I think that one line of rails will take it to a very barren country, and the other to a very fruitful country.

I think it only fair to myself to say that I suppose I was asked to come here on purpose to try and criticise, and I mean to do so. But

C. C.   x

if I had before me an audience of plutocratic sympathies, then I should have the pleasure of speaking much more than I shall to-night in the language of the Fabian Essays.

(*a*) Individualism and Socialism may be considered as names which designate different conditions or organisations of the productive and distributive work of Society : Individualism meaning a competitive system based on private property, such as under certain limitations exists to-day in Europe ; and Socialism meaning a collective organisation of these same functions. Simply for the sake of clearness I shall call these systems and the advocacy of them by the names of Economic Individualism and Economic Socialism respectively.

But (*β*) the two generic names in question carry with them associations belonging to pregnant views of life as a whole ; and Individualism at least may be used to represent a recognised philosophical doctrine of human relations analogous to the theory of matter indicated by the equivalent Greek term Atomism.   And by opposition to this pregnant use of Individualism, and also in virtue of its own obvious derivation, the term Socialism is acquiring, if it did not at first possess, a deeper meaning as a name for a human tendency or aspiration that is operative throughout history, in contrast, we have been told, with " Unsocialism."   To distinguish this more human signification of the words we are discussing from their purely economic usage, I shall specify them when thus employed as Moral Individualism and Moral Socialism respectively, everything being moral, in the philosophical sense, which deals with the value of life as a whole.

Moral Individualism, then, is the materialistic or Epicurean view of life (which, when reasonably interpreted, has a good deal to be said for it);[1] and moral Socialism is the opposite view to this, the view which makes Society the moral essence of the Individual. And I may say at once that for practical purposes of discussion I shall assume this second view to be the right view. In strict philosophy neither of them is right, but only a rational conception which satisfies the demands of both. But there is this great difference between them, that the individual or atomic animal man has a visible body, and therefore we are already quite certain not to deny *his* reality, and we need not further insist upon it by help of a theory; while the moral being of man as a centre of social functions and relations is not visible to the bodily eye, and therefore we do need a theory to insist upon *it*. This shows the ground of philosophical connection between

[1] See Professor Wallace's *Epicureanism*, a beautiful book.

Materialism and Moral Individualism in the tendency to start from what you can most easily see.

For convenience of antithesis, then, I shall speak of Moral Individualism in the sense of actual or theoretical egoism, and Moral Socialism (though this latter is not an accepted expression) in the sense of actual or theoretical recognition that man's moral being lies in his social being. I do not assume that Moral Socialism is the view of morality entertained by Economic Socialists. My object this evening is rather to put the question whether it is so either most naturally, or as a matter of fact. Therefore, what I wish to discuss is the relation between two antitheses: between the antithesis of Economic Individualism to Economic Socialism, and the antithesis of Moral Individualism to Moral Socialism.

There is, I think, a widespread tendency

simply to confuse these two distinctions with one another. The mere name of Socialism evokes an enthusiasm and devotion which show that it is not felt to be merely one system of property-holding, though it is seldom distinctly announced to be anything more; and still less is the question raised, which I am trying to raise just now, *what* more it is. Mr. Kirkup, in the article "Socialism" of the *Encyclopædia Britannica*, has a curiously suggestive passage. He says, "Most of the prevailing Socialism of to-day is based on the frankest and most outspoken revolutionary materialism." Well! Materialism going along with Moral Individualism, this is to say that the two antitheses which we are discussing are *cross-connected*, or at least that Economic Socialism is based on Moral Individualism. But then he continues, "The ethics of Socialism are closely akin to the ethics of Christianity, if not identical with them." This, again, is to say that the two antitheses which I am discussing correspond term for term, or at least that Economic Socialism is based on Moral Socialism. But the question is not pursued after this very suggestive contradiction, which might, one would have thought, have led up to an inquiry how there comes to be this very decided right and left wing in Socialist morality. Even in the Fabian Essays I cannot think that the distinction between Economic and Moral Socialism, with the questions that arise out of it, is quite plainly faced. The sentence on page 148, " The system of property-holding which we call Socialism is not in itself such a life," etc., is therefore refreshing to a philosopher, who has found himself a little bewildered by an implied assumption that two things are the same, about which he wants to know whether they have any connection at all, and if so, what.   The " moral ideas appropriate to Socialism," [1] or " Socialism " as an object of moral judgment,[2] are in another paper rather assumed to be of the nature of what I call Moral Socialism, than shown to be so ; nor do I feel absolutely sure that the author of this paper has made a final choice between the ethical right and left wing.   We all see, indeed, that more general comfort would give morality a better chance, and that industrial co-operation is a good ethical training ; but the statement of these two points hardly amounts to a recognition and treatment of the distinction and connection between Economic Socialism and Moral Socialism.   The pages of this volume, with which, speaking as an ethical student, I feel most at home, are the concluding page and a half of the Essay on Industry

---

[1] p. 127.   [2] p. 104.

under Socialism.[1]   And I do not at all maintain that the connection between economic and moral Socialism, which is there indicated, need be visionary.   Even if I am betrayed into a little polemic, illustrative of what I consider the risks of a false perspective, it is not my object to make an attack.   My object is to get the question recognised in its full difficulty and importance.   I begin, therefore, by stating the *primâ facie* case against a connection between Moral and Economic Socialism.[2]

Morality consists in the presence of some element of the social purpose as a moving idea before the individual mind ; that is, in short, in the social constitution of the individual will.

[1] pp. 168–9.

[2] The Author of the paper on " The Moral Basis of Socialism " says there is no special Socialistic view of the basis of morals.   This may be so, but then I hardly think you could speak of moral ideas appropriate to Socialism. At least, you would have to *make* the connection.

This has been the recognised morality of the Western nations for more than two thousand years, without any essential or fundamental change whatever, the deepening of the individual spirit and intelligence, which has sometimes seemed to tear society apart, having been in every case the germination of a membership in a new social order, sometimes, by illusion, taken for a time to be invisible as well as visible.   Able writers (Mr. Belfort Bax and Mr. Mackay) have absolutely and utterly misunderstood this phenomenon, which they take for a growth of Individualism.

Now, why should Economic Socialism not be favourable to a developed morality of this kind ?   Stated in the abstract, the reason is that it is the same thing in a quite different form, and the general rule is that different forms of the same thing are hostile.   A regular Gallio has no objection to a State Church.

Like Mr. M. Arnold, he thinks that it saves people from becoming too religious. But a man who thinks that the State is itself spiritual is apt to be fanatically opposed to an Establishment. The one form is always seeming to claim the functions of the other, and two different things cannot occupy the same place. It may be answered that all is well so long as they do not claim to occupy the same place, but simply to assist one another as distinct means to the same end. That may be, but then the distinction and the mode of assistance must be very precisely defined.

Morality, as I said, consists in the social purpose working by its own force on the individual will. Economic Socialism is an arrangement for getting the social purpose carried out just not by its own force, but by the force of those compulsory motives or sanctions which are at the command of the public power.

Therefore, *primâ facie*, the normal relation
of the two antitheses of which I spoke would
be that of cross-correspondence.   Economic
Individualism would go with Moral Socialism,
and Moral Individualism (or Egoism) with
Economic Socialism.   If you want to treat
your social units as bricks in a wall or wheels
in a machine, you cannot also and at the same
time treat them as elements in an organism.
Or, it is truer to say, if you can treat them in
these two ways at once, you have solved an
exceedingly difficult problem.   *Primâ facie*,
machinery and morality are quite different
things, and if you are trying to model your
machinery directly upon your morality, it is
long odds that you are guided simply by a
confusion.   Economic Socialism need not presuppose the social organism.   It is, in appearance, a *substitute for* the life of that organism,
intended to operate on the egoistic motives of

individuals for the good of the whole, which cannot, it is assumed, be attained by the moral power of the social purpose.   In this point of view at least it naturally rests on Moral Individualism.   All compulsion through the material necessities of individuals is morally individualistic.   But Economic Individualism does presuppose the social organism, and without it would be the dissolution of society.   It is often alleged that the time of the factory development a hundred years ago was a time of unmixed Economic Individualism.   But this is not so; perhaps the worst evils of that time arose directly from the intentionally lax or "socialistic" Poor Law.   It was the public institutions that for the most part supplied the children who were ill-treated.   Owen's life shows us that by sheer competitive attraction you could *not* get the respectable country people to work under factory conditions.   This suggests a different moral. Economic Individualism assumes that the moral purpose has power to take care of itself throughout the general life of society, and only embodies that purpose in acts of the public power when such acts appear definitely necessary on specific grounds for the support of the private moral will. The Economic Individualist, indeed, who thinks the State to be unconcerned with morality, and to be unjustified in any interference on moral grounds, is a fanatic and doctrinaire, and is the precise counterpart of the Economic Socialist who assumes straight away that collectivism in property naturally implies socialisation of the will. Each of these doctrinaires imagines that the economic and the moral forms of his principle are necessarily coherent with each other, whereas it is much more natural that they should be antagonistic.

If I am asked, "Does this apparent antagonism between Moral and Economic Socialism represent what I believe to be the fact?" I reply, "It represents to me the reality of certain conditions, and my own judgment of any existing or proposed economical machinery would depend upon the degree in which, at the time of its proposal, it should satisfy those conditions."   And these conditions, in accordance with what has been said, may be summed up as the necessity of avoiding the confusion of machinery with morality, on the ground that the moment this confusion begins your Moral Socialism turns automatically into Moral Individualism.

It is therefore the second antithesis—the moral antithesis—and not the first—the economical antithesis—that dominates the question.   Our joint purpose is, as I understand, to find a machinery which will assist morality and not be confounded with it.   To my own mind the great requisite is to acknowledge that all these problems are matters of contrivance and matters of degree. I was electrified, but also edified, not long ago, to find an able writer of the extreme school of doctrinaire Individualists talking about devising new tenures of private property, and about an admirable *substitute for* private property. (He was speaking of Insurance.) This latter phrase is one with which I do not think an Economic Socialist need quarrel. It is perfectly plain and undeniable, I think, that liberty and regulation are increasing side by side as the whole range of life becomes larger, and that what is important is not the relative amount of regulation and of liberty, but the adaptation of both with delicacy and flexibility to the shape and growth of life.

Thus the question assumes the form, not of choosing between two ready-made economic systems, but of developing a specific system to suit the necessities of our life.

From this point of view it is plain that the spirit in which we go to work, the focussing of our picture, the precise line of rail on which we progress, will be simply decisive of the all-important question which I am trying to put before you : " Does Economic Socialism carry with it Moral Socialism or Moral Individualism ? " In the former case it is heaven, and in the latter case it is hell. What I now propose to attempt is to insist further, by help of details both of opinion and of practice, upon the dangerous conditions which I have endeavoured to set out in the above abstract deduction —upon the danger, that is, which lies in the facility of connection between Economic Socialism and Moral Individualism. I want to show, if I can, at how important a parting of the ways Modern Socialism is about to arrive.

1. I quoted from Mr. Kirkup to the effect that there is a great deal of materialism—which means Moral Individualism—in modern Socialism.   Much of this is inherited, no doubt, though not from Robert Owen, and may be passing away.   But much remains, and is inherent—as a *tendency* is inherent—in Economic Socialism.

Take the case in which Economic Socialism frequently appeals to moral considerations ; the polemic against private property.

As a matter of the history of opinion, to begin with, this cuts off Economic Socialism at once from the two greatest expounders of the social organism that the world has ever seen —I mean Aristotle[1] and Hegel.   I do not mention this as if their authority was decisive on practical questions of to-day, because the

---

[1] Newman, Introd. to Aristotle's Politics, 164 and 178.

nature of property has changed and is continually changing. But it is important, when Economic Socialists begin—as I am glad to see they are beginning—to speak about the social organism, to bear in mind that a radical and fundamental polemic against private property is quite incompatible with any legitimate affiliation to those who gave us this spiritual principle. What about Plato? it may be asked. Well! Aristotle's complaint against him, reduced to modern terms, is that Plato had needlessly destroyed the social organism by trusting to machinery instead of morality. On the other hand, I grant that private property, as Aristotle would have it, is a different thing from ours. Now, with reference to Hegel, one notices at times a tendency in Economic Socialism to be a little proud of a somewhat doubtful affiliation to him. It is quite true that Karl Marx used the forms of the dialectic with extraordinary ingenuity, and one hopes that the deeper spiritual ideas of Hegel's teaching are passing, and will pass, more and more into the temper of nineteenth-century reformers. It is, moreover, true that Hegel denounced as a blunder the idea which I have stigmatised as characteristic of doctrinaire Individualism: the idea that the public recognition of moral purposes is necessarily fatal to individual moral freedom. So far, an Economic Socialist can count upon Hegel as against a doctrinaire Individualist. But when you read Hegel's treatment of private property, and realise the depth and complexity of the moral problem to which he regards it as the answer, and then pass from that treatment to the view which regards it as the embodiment of individual cupidity and indolence, I think every one must be aware that one has passed to another and not a higher moral atmosphere.

I hope I shall not weary you too much if I quote a characteristic page from Hegel's *Philosophy of Right* " :—

" As, in property, my will is made real for me as a personal will—that is, as the will of an individual — property is characteristically *private* property ; while common property, such as in its nature can be severally possessed, bears the character of a dissoluble combination, in which I can choose or not choose to leave my share.

" The use of the elements " [I suppose he means air and water—he might have meant land but for the next sentence] " is incapable of being made a private possession. The agrarian laws at Rome contain a conflict between collectivism and private property in land ; the latter necessarily gained the day, as the more

---

[1] *Rechtsphil.*, p. 81.

reasonable factor in the social system, although at the expense of other rights. Family trust property contains a factor which is opposed to the right of personality, and therefore to that of private property. But the rules which deal with private property may be subordinated to higher spheres of right, to a corporation or to the State, as in the case when ownership is vested in a so-called moral person—property in mortmain. However, such exceptions must not be founded in caprice or private interest, but only in the rational organisation of the State.

" The idea of Plato's Republic contains as a general principle the injustice against the person of making him incapable of holding private property. The idea of a pious or friendly or even compulsory fraternity of human beings with community of goods, and the banishment of the principle of private property, may easily occur to a habit of thought which mistakes the nature of spiritual freedom and of right, and does not apprehend them in their definite factors. As for the moral or religious point of view, Epicurus deterred his friends from organising such a community of goods, when they thought of doing so, precisely on the ground that to do so would indicate mistrust, and that people who mistrust one another are not friends.

" *Note.* In property my will takes the shape of a person. Now a person is something in particular; therefore the property is the personification of this will. As I give my will existence by means of property, property in its turn must have the attribute of being this in particular, *i.e.* mine. This is the important doctrine of the necessity of private property. If exceptions are made by the State, it is it alone that can make them; and often in our own days it has *restored* private property.

So, for example, many nations have rightly abolished the monasteries, because in the last resort a collective institution has no such right to property as the person has."

Now if it is maintained that the reasonable necessity which in Hegel's view demanded the existence of private property can now be met by a modification of the private ownership system, or even by some different system, that might fairly be urged without breaking your line of descent from idealistic or organic philosophy which is one with moral Socialism. But if you say that private ownership is, and always has been, simply the expression of individual greed, and the desire to be indolent and incompetent, then, by a phenomenon very common in controversy, you arouse a well-grounded suspicion that you are ascribing this foundation —the foundation of Moral Individualism—to the normal life of humanity, simply because it is the foundation on which your own views ultimately rest, and you are aware of no other. It appears to me that Economic Socialism wavers between these two attitudes, and that the latter, the polemic against private ownership, altogether and as such, betrays, as Hegel implies, an entire blindness to the essential elements of the social organism, which can only exist as a structure of free individual wills, each entertaining the social purpose in an individual form appropriate to its structural position and organic functions. It is perhaps a platitude, but one which we all of us are perpetually failing to apply, that throughout life the attempt to realise an abstraction as an abstraction is self-contradictory and a ruinous failure. To aim directly at pleasure for pleasure's sake means failure in happiness; to aim at duty for duty's sake means failure in morality; to aim at beauty for beauty's sake means failure in fine art; to aim at truth for truth's sake (the net result) means failure in science; to aim at the general purpose for the sake of the purpose as general means failure in social reform. I confess that I believe modern Economic Socialism to rest *in part* on this ineradicable confusion. "We want a general good life; let us make a law that there shall be a general good life." But, precisely as other-worldliness arises from the religious impulse when embodied in a mechanical form, so, and for identically the same reasons, does Moral Individualism arise automatically from the impulse of Moral Socialism when embodied in a mechanical form. You must let the individual make his will a reality in the conduct of his life, in order that it may be possible for him consciously to entertain the social purpose as a constituent of his will. Without these conditions there is no social organism and no Moral Socialism. This is the meaning of the doctrines of Aristotle and Hegel, and this it is which the ethical left wing of the Socialists, alluded to by Mr. Kirkup, appears to me wholly to ignore.

2. But the question is not one merely of the history of opinion or of ethical formulas. If it were, it would be too purely academic for even a philosophical discussion before the Fabian Society. It is one also of practical tendency —a difficult thing to grasp and bring home in detail ; but I propose to indicate by one or two instances what I mean.

a. I have spoken of the theory of private property. Now, theoretical attitude communicates a bias, as every one knows, to particular perceptions. I do not think I ever noticed a Socialist alluding, except with derision, to the duties of property. Of course you may maintain that you are right in fact—that these duties are a negligible quantity, or a ridiculous

pretence. Time forbids me to argue upon the
proper interpretation of this state of things,
which indisputably exists in great measure.
But, however this attitude may be justified, I
want to point out what it amounts to. The
long and short of it is that those who speak in
this way do not really believe in Moral Socialism. To those who believe in Moral Socialism
the source of a payment makes no difference to
the duty it involves. So long as one can live,
the duty of working for Society is imperative ;
if one has more than enough to live on, that is
a charge—something to work with, to organise,
to direct. Property is mediate payment with
responsibility ; salary is immediate payment.
I never saw it recognised by a Socialist that
property could be a burden. I wish to avoid
overstraining, and I will admit against myself
that my own class is probably the most selfish
of all ; that is, the class which has enough to

tempt it into a little luxury, but not enough to constitute a notable responsibility and public charge.   But this defect of a limited class does not justify a want of faith which misconstrues a fundamental factor of human morality.   And this defect of faith is radical, and is connected directly with Economic Socialism.   It means that the reason for equalising opportunity is not merely that you want to give nine-tenths of the people a better chance than they have now—to level up to the highest standard to which you may in practice be able to level up —but that you do not believe any one will work unless his livelihood depends upon it. Now I cannot fight the battle of all human nature in five minutes; but I will lay down one principle as tolerably certain, and it is this: a man who will not work if his livelihood is secure without it will be an uncommonly bad workman if his livelihood depends upon it.

Practically speaking, this whole view is to my observation false; and, technically speaking, it unquestionably is Moral Individualism. Here I am glad to have on my side the concluding pages of the Essay on " Industry under Socialism," which represents the ethical right wing, and, as I hope, the future of Socialistic ideas.

β. I have said that many Socialists speak as if they did not *believe in* the socialisation of the will. It is a corollary from this that they should not care about the socialisation of the will.

There are indications that the natural connection of Economic Socialism with Moral Individualism tends to realise itself in this respect also. I will adduce some instances which may at least explain my meaning.

(i.) I admit that I have not found in the Fabian Essays the direct disparagement of *thrift* which I anticipated that I should find.

The only allusion to the subject which I have observed is the remark that thrift is preached by extravagant people, which doubtless is true. Otherwise, I think, the subject is somewhat severely let alone. I believe that I am not mistaken in saying that the inculcation of thrift is looked upon with coldness, if not with aversion, by modern Economic Socialism. It is said, and I do not know that Socialists would desire to deny it, that the introduction of Post Office Savings Banks into Prussia was prevented by the influence of Lassalle's movement upon the Government, the then Director of the Post Office being anxious to introduce them.

Now I am well aware of two things: first, that there are different kinds of thrift—speaking roughly, the selfish kind and the unselfish kind; and secondly, I am aware that there is no greater deterrent against saving than the impossibility of saving enough to be of any use.   This is an every-day experience among the less wealthy class of professional men.   But yet I appeal with confidence to any one who has practical familiarity with the character and distresses of the working class, to say whether experience does not show that thrift among them goes with unselfishness and a sense of duty, and unthrift with selfishness and self-indulgence.   I would rather, I think, have on my soul the sin which has been committed by Englishmen in high places, of speaking lightly of intemperance, than the sin of having let fall a word of discouragement for that foresight and self-control which is, and always must be, the ground and medium of all Moral Socialism. I see no ultimate discrepancy between the purposes of Economic Socialism and this elementary factor of morality.   I do see a *primâ facie* antagonism between the two, in so far as Economic Socialism rests upon the individualistic fallacy of thinking that you can maintain a moral structure without maintaining the morality which is the cohesion of its units. It should be clearly understood that thrift, in the shape of a resolution to bear at least your own burdens, is not a selfish but an unselfish quality, and is the first foundation and the well-known symptom of a tendency, not to Moral Individualism, but to Moral Socialism. This point is not met by saying that it is hard to save on 19s. a week. We are speaking of a quality in moral character, which determines the happiness or misery of those who possess or do not possess it, in a way that goes far deeper into life than by mere success or failure in laying by a sum of money. The man who looks ahead and tries to provide for bearing his own burden is the man who can appreciate a social purpose, and who cares for the happiness of those dependent on him. Him, if he fails in part you may safely help for a time; if he fails altogether by exceptional misfortune, you should, I incline to think, distinguish him in your Poor Law treatment from the man who shows no signs of such a disposition.   But to try and take away from him the one thing on which his manliness and his chance of happiness depend by speaking lightly of the duty of carrying at least one's own burden, betrays a standpoint which is not that of Moral Socialism.

(ii.) I turn from a question of feeling and mode of speech to a question more directly practical.   In speaking of the present Poor Law system, a chief fault to which a Socialist calls attention is harshness of administration and desire to save the rates.   Now, that there was great brutality in Poor Law administration not very long ago, that signs of such brutality appear to crop up still from time to time, that defects arising from foolish economy are alleged against some Poor Law schools, and that the system of large district schools may require reconsideration,—all this appears to me to be true. And it is plain that sensible kindliness, the greatest possible care for education, and a differential treatment of those whose misfortunes are special and unavoidable, should be principles pervading the administration of the Poor Law.[1]

Nevertheless, after all these allowances are made in justification of the Socialist criticism, I should say that it points in precisely the wrong direction. These matters, indeed, cannot really be discussed on a quantitative basis; nothing in actual life can be so treated. In all these social problems it is not really either a less or a more that is wanted; it is something *different*; something which would be more in

---

[1] See Preface.

some cases, and less in others. But if I must use roughly approximate terms of quantity, to which popular treatment always inclines, I should say that what is wanted is to lessen the amount of Poor Law assistance; to make the administration not more lax, but more strict; not more lenient, but more harsh. I observe that in the Essay on " Industry under Social-ism " it is contemplated without a shudder that those who, in a reformed social system, and with a fair chance of work before them, de-liberately refuse to support themselves, might without injustice be left to starve. Now the complication of deserved and undeserved calamity represented by our pauperism to-day cannot be thus regarded as meriting strictly penal treatment. On the other hand, the moral requirement suggested by the passage seems to me too low. We require more of a man than the willingness to work as an alternative to bare starvation.   We require that in laying his plan of life, and not simply with a view to his own possible disaster, he should be guided by the principle that he will never become a burden to others like himself.   Therefore you must judge these cases not merely by their present misery, but by their past selfish folly.   And therefore we must treat the failure in self-support as something which, though we dare not now bring it, as the more socialistic Athenians did, within the compass of the penal law, yet demands not only the pity but also the reprobation of society.   I look upon the exceptional case of destitution by pure misfortune in a manner analogous to that in which I regard a legal offender who is free, by some accident, from moral culpability.   These cases there partly is, and more completely might be, a mode of hindering or of alleviating.   Here is the sphere of individual kindliness and skill.

What do I want, then, to bring the thing to an issue? I want all ordinary cases of destitution to be treated in the workhouse, with gentleness and human care, but under strict regulation and not on a high scale of comfort. I want all cases of exceptional misfortune, which has finally frustrated foresight and persistent effort, to be treated by private skill and judgment, apart from the Poor Law, through the dutiful care of relatives or neighbours. I want the State supplementation of the resources of those who are poor but not destitute, known as out-relief, to cease altogether. Here I must add a word to show the special bearing of this on my philosophical contention. You cannot restore a broken life by mechanical support. This deep and subtle relation between the character and circumstances shows itself not in one form but in many forms of evil which arise from the attempt.   There is physical evil—this supplementation of resources, owing to the constant fear of deception, is never adequate, and actually causes the partial or entire starvation which it is intended to avert.   There is economical evil—the rate in aid of wages; I need not enlarge on this.   There is moral evil—the confusion of responsibility between the individual and Society as a whole.   " I have paid rates for many years," a labourer out of work once said to me—" why should I not have my relief simply by asking for it ? "   The Economic Socialism of out-relief had driven this poor man into Moral Individualism ; seeing the fund to which he contributed used to tide over the difficulties of the improvident, he thought that the State intended, in part at least, to take the duty of providence off his shoulders ; his will was confused, and his life very probably ruined.   No money will make up to a man for a broken mainspring in his social will.

There is one fundamental objection—or, rather, one incisive retort, for I cannot admit that it is an objection—which a Socialist may make to all this argument. He may say, " Is not, at least, inherited or unearned property an equally pernicious subvention to the rich as out-relief to the poor ? "

I point out one distinction, and then give my general answer. Property is within the owner's control and is a permission to him to choose his work—of course an enormous indulgence. But Poor Law relief is not in the recipient's control, is a payment for idleness, and is not sufficient to set the life free to choose work. A large pension or gift of property to a man not yet demoralised would probably do no harm. This is the paradox about doles already known to Aristotle, and recognised by expert philanthropists to-day. Great expenditure which "sets a man up" does not as a rule demoralise; it is the little chronic subventions, which give no freedom and are actually consequent upon the failure of the social will, that cause demoralisation.

I do not think it can be denied that property *may* have a similar effect. Wherever it distracts from one social vocation, without forming the basis of another, there it operates as out-relief pure and simple, and there the strictures of the Fabian Essays have full application. With this concession, I pass from the distinction which I had to draw between property and out-relief, to the general answer which I make to the retort which consists in comparing them.

The answer is simply this : that two blacks do not make a white, and that the identification of property with out-relief, if established, might be a good argument for abolishing property, but could not possibly be a plea in favour of out-relief.

(iii.) And with out-relief I class all inadequate treatment of the symptom of social evil which is known as poverty. I mention especially large-scale organisations for free dinners at popular schools, and large-scale arrangements for giving employment to the casual unemployed.

In all these matters the same tendency is traceable—the tendency to adapt machinery to dealing with a large effect, superficially apparent, without distinguishing the very different classes of cause, demanding different means for their neutralisation, which concur in producing this large apparent effect. Especially in the problem of feeding the children who attend school every case needs special and separate investigation. It is certainly sometimes possible to persuade parents to pay for food supplied to their children, who before permitted it to be given to them for nothing. I have seen this done, on a very small scale indeed, and in this case there has been not only a physical gain to the child, but also a moral gain to the parents. I cannot strongly enough protest that to us who believe in the socialisation of the will, the treatment of these questions by large-scale machinery assumes the aspect, not of sympathy and charity, but of negligence and cruelty. Discrimination, if guided merely by the test of the child's immediate need, means on the whole that the wrong people are helped and the right people are not helped. To this I should prefer, if it were the only alternative, that all children should be given a free meal without discrimination; in which case there would not be the peculiar extra aggravation that just precisely in proportion as people fail to do their duty, the public does it for them. I may add, that under the present social system these advantages probably send up the rents in the neighbourhoods where they are provided, so that the happy landlord pockets the weekly value of the child's dinner. This, however, is not an argument that can ultimately carry weight with Socialists. It should weigh with everybody for the present, I think.

(iv.) It is plain, moreover, that Economic Socialism is anything but warmly disposed towards productive co-operation, the existence of which, as distinct from joint-stock shopkeeping, would hardly be gathered from the reference to the subject in the Fabian Essay on The Industrial Basis of Socialism. Although Dr. Ingram's opinion [1] is evidently, like the Fabian Essayist's, that no great importance belongs

---

[1] *Encyclopædia Britannica*, Article " Political Economy."

even to productive co-operation, yet it is worth observing that in the passage to which the Fabian Essay alludes he is discussing Cairnes' view to the contrary, and the modern economists whom he quotes against Cairnes are not quite spoken of as " modern economists in general."   This is a matter of no real importance, except as an indication of a well-known Socialistic attitude of mind—of what almost amounts to a dread of all processes that chiefly depend on the socialisation of the will; because, I suppose, the primary antagonism between Economic and Moral Socialism is instinctively felt, without being theoretically demonstrated.   The success of productive co-operation, I take it, in view of the modern successful management of joint-stock companies, is simply and solely an affair of the workman's industrial and moral education.[1]

---

[1] I leave this passage as it was delivered.   Miss Potter's

(v.) The word education brings me to my last set of illustrations, which are on ground more familiar to me. The Economic Socialist is willing, as I rejoice to see, to spend money on the children, but I do not see that, since the time of Robert Owen, his eyes have been very sharp to detect the real needs of education. Owen proposed that there should be national training colleges for teachers—a truly statesmanlike proposal, which I wish was included in the platform of some party to-day. Probably, in his sympathy with Lancaster, Owen may have been careless about the size of the division entrusted to a single teacher, on which both Bell and Lancaster had absurd ideas. On this question experience has taught

work on "The Co-operative Movement" has probably intensified the attitude towards "Productive" Co-operation, which I refer to, but at the same time assigns ethical motives for the view which she adopts.

us much, and to double the present staff of teachers, at least in our infant schools, is a very moderate proposal. It would be much more important to give a piano to every Board School than to give " free dinners " to the children.[1] It is heart-breaking to see the children marching to the mere clapping of hands.

And one thing more is necessary to sound education. You must carry the parents along with you. There is nothing in this contrary to Economic Socialism ; it seems to be successfully attempted in Godin's Familistère at Guise. But, like the other matters I have referred to, you can only do it by real enthusiasm for the socialisation of the individual

---

[1] I must insist that this sentence does *not* mean that pianos, which I rejoice to see are to be given, are more important than the proper care and nourishment of school children. If I said that to pay for making school life happier is better than to pay parents to neglect their children, the saying might seem less hard.

will. No machinery can effect it. You must
make it your duty, and inspire your managers
with the zeal for this duty, to get the parents
interested, until at last they come to know and
care and act effectively in controlling the
education of their children. The thing can be
done. I have seen a beginning made—a very
trifling one.

(vi.) And as a final instance, I would say
one word upon the ideal, often connected with
Economic Socialism, of beautiful surroundings
of life and the interchangeability of labour.
Here again, I believe, we find, mingled with
much sound insight, a theoretical confusion, the
pursuit of an abstraction. Socialists always
say, and quite rightly, that you cannot go back.
Well, for that reason I think that you can
never again be free from the intellectuality
of modern life; and therefore I think that
material beauty and splendour will never again

have their old importance in our lives. We shall have, I trust, a devotion to beauty—probably a deeper beauty than before—and shall learn to avoid the sordid and hideous; but when a lad can buy Shakespeare for a shilling and read him in a garret, it is impossible that we should ever again absolutely depend for our chief spiritual nutriment on the beauty of the more sensuous arts and crafts. I do not underrate these great goods of life; I am often accused of valuing them too highly. I only want to point out that the whole basis of mind and society is now definitely intellectual and ideal, and in the historical idea we have explicitly what the artistic tradition used to represent implicitly. " Literature is dirt-cheap,"[1] and every one can read it; and though I cannot doubt that the fine arts of sense-perception

---

[1] Fabian Essays.

C.C. A A

have a future, yet the modern mind is so deep and so strong that it can bear, and to some extent must bear, the divorce from sensuous beauty, which would have killed the ancient Greek or mediæval Italian.

This brings me to the question of the interchangeability of labour. Here, as elsewhere, I do not think that Economic Socialism appreciates the depth of individuality which is necessary in order to contain, in a moral form, the modern social purpose. Each unit of the social organism has to embody his relations with the whole in his own particular work and will; and in order to do this the individual must have a strength and depth in himself proportional to and consisting of the relations which he has to embody. Thus, if the individual in ancient Greece was like a centre to which a thousand threads of relation were attached, the individual in modern Europe might be compared to a centre on which there hang many, many millions. You cannot go back to a simple world, in which the same man can conquer all knowledge, or be versed in all practice. If all are, as we hope, to share in the gains achieved by each, it can only be through the gigantic and ever-increasing labour by which every worker takes account, in his work, of its import for all. There should not be castes of workers, if caste means a social division ; there must be classes of workers, because the increasing material of human knowledge and endeavour will more and more consume the entire lives and thoughts of those upon whom its burden falls.

This argument is not directed against rational provisions for doing away with unskilled labour, or for imposing some public activity on every citizen in excess of his normal vocation. It is directed against the idea that work becomes useful by being popular in the sense of being unspecialised and superficial; whereas it is plain to all who know, that only thoroughness can impart universal significance, and that the claim upon the student, and artist, and scientist will more and more take the form, " It is expedient that one man should die for the people." This is very far from being a selfish contention on the student's part. In an age of universal education, the student's services, more than those of any one else, will be obtainable, should society so choose, at starvation wages.

I need not multiply these illustrations. I have said enough to make my meaning clear. Economic Individualism and Economic Socialism are both obviously on the move, each of them desiring to make good its differently-founded claims to harmonise with Moral Socialism, which is the only thing for which any healthy human being, at the bottom of his heart, cares a single straw. The Moral Socialist looks on, confident that the forces of human nature will make the reality prevail, but not all unwilling to co-operate with those forces wherever he can find a purchase. And such a purchase would be found if it were possible to convince the Economic Socialist that in dealing with the social organism he is dealing with a structure whose units are the characters of men and women ; and that in so far as he neglects to base his arrangements on the essence of character—that is, on the social or moral will—so far he is not dealing with the social organism as an organism, but rather as a machine—that is to say, from the point of view, not of Moral Socialism, but of Moral Individualism.

XI.

LIBERTY AND LEGISLATION. [1]

Among the antagonistic ideas of human progress which confront one another at the present time, there is no more remarkable pair of seeming opposites than the demand for completer liberty and the desire for more thorough-going legislation.

Both of these aspirations appear characterstic of our era; while by one party to the controversy at least, the two tendencies are regarded as absolutely incompatible with each other. It is curious that those who represent

---

[1] Delivered at South Place Chapel, Finsbury.

the opposition in its most ultimate form, the Anarchist and the Socialist respectively, have some inkling that there may be a meeting of the extremes ; but Stuart Mill and Fitzjames Stephen, or Mr. Auberon Herbert and Sir John Lubbock must be regarded as absolute irreconcilables.

I want to consider with you to-day this very astonishing divergence of opinion, in order to ascertain, if we can, the real direction of the movement which can give rise to such very different estimates. For no one is so wholly a pessimist as to entertain an aspiration which he admits to be fundamentally in contradiction with the whole set and tide of human endeavour. What a man believes to be right, that he believes, in one way or another, at bottom or in the long run, to be tending to come to pass.

And to clear the issue, I would say that I

am, as far as at all possible, using the word liberty in its every-day acceptation, that of freedom from felt coercion, and power to do what you please. I do not desire to cut the knot by referring to the more philosophical idea of freedom as submission to a noble law. I want to begin by using those notions of liberty and coercion which unquestionably do hold a place in our daily judgments respecting politics and society. And for that purpose I will take them as I find them; as they meet us from day to day in the great practical and theoretical controversy between those who with Mr. Spencer think all politics an evil, and those who, like most of ourselves, assent with more or less conviction to the overwhelming necessity which produces year by year a larger and larger statute book. If, however, I should be driven by the sheer force of logical continuity to appeal before I close to a somewhat loftier standard of liberty, it will be only because we shall have found, that the higher liberty is rooted in the lower, and that the lower must necessarily grow upwards into the higher.

Now philosophers are often accused of not taking a side.   It is their business to reconcile and explain ; and they often cause perplexity by seeming to pronounce that if A is right from one point of view, B is right from another and C from a third, and so on through the whole alphabet.   To-day, however, though I cannot but try to reconcile and explain, yet I hope very distinctly to take a side.   For I hold that the view of the anti-governmental theorist is not merely an imperfect view, but is a misapprehension of an imperfect view.   I do not consider that it is the true balance or counterpart to the convictions of those who believe in social authority.   I do not acknowledge that it represents the great and valuable principles of effective individual development, of spontaneity, of robustness, of originality. It would be an imperfect conception to suppose that the largest possible liberty of individual action was the only desirable object and standard of life. Nobility and order would be elements neglected by such an ideal. But the view that social compulsion is bad in principle is not even this demand for liberty, but is a misapprehension of this demand. It is not one remove, but two removes from truth. It not merely aims at an imperfect ideal of freedom, but points the wrong road to this imperfect ideal. Every illusion is founded on a fact, but the illusion may consist in ascribing the fact to conditions precisely the reverse of those which really produce it. This I believe to be the case with the facts on which the anti-governmental theorists base their opinions.

What, in the first place, are these facts ?   I suppose they are such as the following :—

We expect in modern life, and in some measure we obtain, a progressively greater range and choice of action, and a decrease of certain kinds of restriction to which our fore-fathers submitted.   We should not stand having the fashion of our dress, or our power of travelling about, or our religion, or the hour by which we must be indoors in the evening, prescribed for us by law.   And in as far as it is true that most of our fellow-citizens can practically get no choice or variety in their lives, we say that this is a burning shame, and that our system is so far a failure.   We will not submit to any difference being made by the general law between one man and another, and we are rapidly coming to object to a difference being made between the rights of men and women.

It is on such facts and feelings as these that I suppose the case against governmental interference must be rested, in so far as it is not merely an inference from the non-moral nature of acts done under direct coercion, to which I have to refer again.

Is it a right interpretation of such facts and feelings as I have mentioned to say that the modern movement is, at bottom, against compulsion and towards *merely* voluntary association ?

I answer No ; it is not a right interpretation ; it is a wrong one. People who hold these views are sometimes called Individualists ; and no doubt they mean to be Individualists ; but they *are* nothing of the kind. They are pretty well such friends to the individual as the British Admiral was to the British engineer who was alleged to be serving under coercion in a Peruvian man-of-war. The Admiral, so the story goes, let fly a Whitehead torpedo at the Peruvian ship, and if he had hit it the oppressed individual would have been liberated from his oppressors by going to the bottom along with them.

Theorists of this type do not know what the individual is, and in trying to free him from tyranny they are dismembering him. But if they are wrong in maintaining that the true progress of modern society is to cut the cords of social authority, what are we to say about the phenomena on which they must rely, and which I have admitted to be real and to be welcome? Do not these phenomena show an increase of liberty, and do they not therefore show a decrease of restriction?

I reply that they do show an increase of liberty, but they do not show a decrease of restriction. An increase of one quantity involves a decrease of another only when the total of the two quantities taken together is limited. And this wholly false assumption is at the root of the entirely erroneous view, which in my judgment Mr. Auberon Herbert —I mention his name in particular, because his trumpet gives no uncertain sound—which Mr. Auberon Herbert takes with regard to life. If life could be compared to a limited space, like a box, and liberty and compulsion could be compared to sets of white and black balls to be put into it, then no doubt the more liberty, the less compulsion, and *vice versâ*. But so much depends upon your metaphor! Just put the case that life could better be compared to a tree, that liberty might then be expressed as the access of the leaves to light and air, and restriction or compulsion might be typified by the strong fixtures of the stem and branches. Then it is pretty plain that the more compulsion, the more liberty, and *vice versâ.* Try again : let life be like a great city, let its liberty correspond to the variety, number, and area of the rooms, and its element of compulsion to the walls of the buildings. Here again it would seem that liberty and compulsion must increase together.

It is not the fact, then, that increased liberty means decreased restriction. But it does mean some peculiarity in the character of restriction which distinguishes modern life from the life of our forefathers, and of barbarous or savage peoples. It is now a commonplace that the life of savages, instead of being as free as the bird in the air, is hedged in on every side with idle belief and groundless prohibition. What is it that in contrast with this cramped and fettered condition constitutes the freedom of modern life ?

The quality of freedom does not depend on the great or small amount of social compulsion and fixed enactment, but on two characteristics which belong to life as a whole; and these are :—

First, its comprehensiveness, and secondly, its rationality.

1. In the first place, then, the range of possible actions presented to the individual for his choice becomes, as society develops, more and more comprehensive. His liberty, therefore, in the common straight-forward sense of doing what he pleases, becomes greater and greater. And the yearly Acts of Parliament, forming a thick volume, to which for the purpose of our argument, we ought in strictness to add all by-laws passed and orders made under Parliamentary powers, do not militate against this liberty, but are the conditions of its existence.

Consider, for example, the great province of legal conveyance and contract, which pervades all the relations of civilized life. The form of a contract or a will is an arbitrary matter. It is of no real importance what are the conditions of validity imposed upon such acts, so long as they are easily fulfilled and definitely recognisable. So that by the *fiat* of a general authority, which settles once for all what the conditions of these acts are to be, the facility of transacting business is enormously increased. A compulsory enactment is here the very organ of an enlarged liberty. It is worth while to mention the special example of compulsory registration conferring an absolute title to land, a measure of coercion so drastic that we have hitherto been afraid to enact it, and yet it would at one blow make the transfer of land a comparatively simple matter, and therefore open up far greater possibilities in the way of buying and selling real property. This is an exceedingly striking example of the relation, which I am trying to illustrate, between liberty and compulsion.

And so it is throughout. Everything that you can do involves a number of things that you cannot do, and the restrictions of a larger life are more numerous than the restrictions of a smaller life, just as the branches of a great tree are more numerous than those of a herb or bush.

If we go through all the great departments of legislation, we shall find the same thing. Everywhere the coercive restrictions are simply conditions and results of immense extensions of life, immense enlargements of the range of possible action. Our manufacturing system, our commercial system, our railway system, our educational system, must all of them have a definite shape sanctioned by the community. The practical question, whether we are over- or under-legislating, touches only a small proportion of the enactments relating to these great departments of life. It is quite impossible that completely new outgrowths of civilisation or complete transformations of our mode of doing business should fail to be registered under a social sanction. How could railways be made without Acts of Parliament or worked without by-laws? And how could parties of working men, or indeed of professional men or women, go to Venice or to Florence in the Easter holidays without railways? Is it not plain that authority and liberty are here again inseparably interwoven?

But, secondly, there is something further; modern life is becoming not only more comprehensive, but more rational. There is a change in the kind of restrictions which we expect and are willing to put up with. It used to be said, for example, that the tendency of modern law was from status to contract, that is from a classification of persons determined beforehand by the legal system, according to birth, to arrangements or contracts made by themselves at pleasure, and only ratified by the community. Granting that this were so, as to a great extent it certainly has been, it is only a change, though a most important one, in the *kind* of compulsion, for all contracts rest, as all status rests, on legal compulsion—and then it is perhaps doubtful whether change is so exclusively in this direction as has been thought.

I do not myself believe that it is possible to lay down any single definite direction which must be taken by the course of legislative enactment as time goes on. And by giving my reason for not believing it possible, I shall explain, so far as I can see how to explain, the actual positive process by which the nature of compulsion comes to be modified.

Human life—this seems to me to be the

central truth upon this question—is a thing which at any given moment has a certain shape and certain properties. The shape and properties vary in the most subtle way, and grow more and more complex ; but they are always there, and can be gradually learnt by reason and experience. Now the shape of life is the outward expression of its reasonableness or equilibrium—the arrangement of its parts and of their functions, so that they work. And when I say that compulsion changes on the whole by gaining in rationality, I mean that it becomes more and more identified with the support and maintenance of this shape or balance of life. The beauty of a tree depends very largely on the remarkable ingenuity with which its branches keep out of one another's way. Social compulsion gains the same sort of merit as this, in as far as it supports the figure and balance of the social organism, without causing its parts to thwart or impede one another.

Compare it for a moment to a prop supporting a tree, or to the timbers of a house—as it is something done on purpose, and not unconscious like the tree's own growth.   Now a prop, or a bit of scaffolding, or a timber in a house, is reasonably arranged when it is in the right place according to the shape and function of the thing it has to support.   You may put a stout pole under the branch of a tree as a prop, and it will be of use and do no harm.   But if you tie even a slender stick across the leading shoot you will ruin your tree for ever ; and in the same way in building a house you do not put your beams across the windows or through the chimneys, but you put them out of the way.

This illustrates what I mean by compulsion becoming reasonable.   I mean that it becomes adapted in detail to the particular definite shape and balance of civilized life, so as to support it, and not interfere with it. And then it is not felt as compulsion. For example, we say, quite truly, that nowadays Government ought not to interfere with private opinion or with free discussion about politics and religion. This is quite agreed upon by every one worth mentioning, but the reason is apt to be misunderstood. It is not that Government does not care about our opinions, nor that Government has no right to touch our opinions; it is that reasonable opinion is a thing of a particular kind, and cannot be beneficially affected by direct coercion or by interfering with discussion. It is like a flower; you cannot make it grow right by pulling it about. We have found this out by very sad experience, and now we can see it by common sense; and so it has become a practical rule that Government is not to interfere directly with free discussion and with individual opinion. But if you coupled this practical rule with a general principle, and said that Government has nothing to do with the reasonableness and morality of its citizens, then that is simple non-sense. The truth of the matter is that the public authority, like any individual, must learn to go to work in the right way; and the right way is only learnt by experience of the needs and functions of society.

And in fact, if you say that the public author-ity is to do nothing in any way interfering with opinion and religious discussion, that is simply not true. Government ought to do a great deal, and does a great deal, for the formation of rational opinion and a moral temper on the part of individuals. It interferes by pub-lic education and the means of education, by putting its special information at the dis-posal of public opinion—the English blue books are an unequalled repository of social and economical knowledge only obtained through compulsory powers—and again by the definite line which the public authority is forced to take on questions of social and moral importance, and by forcibly removing temptation where this can be done. We think, once more, that you ought not to establish any Church. No not *now*, because there is no Church that represents the nation—but it was not always wrong to establish a Church; if the nation wanted one it had a right to have one, and if it does not want one it has a right not to have one, that is all, as it seems to me, that can be said in general about it. All these, and I might add the question of interference with trade, are matters in which we have gradually and painfully learnt how, in what particular way, to interfere without doing harm. We interfere now with trade rather by Factory Acts than by Protection, as the needs of the community take

a shape which demands this kind of interference.   But there is no general moral principle which condemns protection;   there is
not even any general moral principle which
condemns taxing the community for the benefit of a class;   on the contrary, we are at
present very largely doing so, and whether
wisely or not depends I think entirely on how
the administration is performed.   The future
of the Poor Law is quite obscure.   All must
depend on the effect with which it is found to
work.   General principles cannot decide such
a question beforehand, because you cannot tell
beforehand under *what* general principle the
concrete result may practically come.   You
have to watch and observe and mould your law
so as while preventing the last results of destitution, not to break the springs of character.
We are not indeed likely, I suppose, ever
again to tax the whole community for the

benefit of a *richer* class ; that is because our concrete idea of the purpose and working of the community has changed in detail, and we do not now believe in any heaven-born governors, whom it is a privilege to the community to support.

Thus, then, I repeat, liberty, in the plainest and simplest sense of the word, does not depend on the absence of legislation, but on the comprehensiveness and reasonableness of life. The coercive power of England or of the United States of America, which, with all their faults, are the two freest countries that the world has ever seen, is such as would have broken the most tyrannical despotisms of the ancient world as a Nasmyth hammer crushes a walnut shell. But the amount of this coercive power no more interferes with our liberty than the strength of your floor interferes with the serviceableness of your house. It is not weakness of the public power, but its adaptation on which freedom depends. What we have therefore to do, is not to trouble ourselves about the more or less of legislative interference; but, living out our lives in some particular honest endeavour, and making those general arrangements which spring out of obvious felt necessities, to call in the social power whenever and wherever good cannot be done without it, and can be done with its help. And we must remember that by the infinite subtlety of modern organization the social power is becoming in practice what it always has been in theory, simply the expression of ourselves. Where does the social power reside? Who are its agents? Where does its responsibility rest? On the House of Commons and the County Council only? Oh no! not at all. Show me a man or woman in the full enjoyment of physical and intellectual capacities, who is in no sense an agent of the social power, and I will show you a man or woman who is not doing his or her duty. There is no longer a class of governors and a class of governed. I am not referring merely to the parliamentary and municipal franchise, important as are the duties which these lay upon us. I am referring partly to that detailed subdivision of authority and function by which the power and right of the community are in every district in the hands of a great army of officials, both paid and unpaid, and to a great extent of ourselves, and partly, and more especially, to the great force of public opinion, which is all that gives value or reasonableness to law. Every one who forms a clear and honest judgment on matters that concern him and his neighbours is putting into operation the social power.

Thus mere actual liberty, variety of possible action, is in no way opposed to extensive social coercion.   Still less are strength and originality of character endangered by legislation.   There is a commonplace set of fallacies, by which the great qualities of human nature are confused with their caricatures : character with perversity, originality with eccentricity, knowledge of the world with experience of its seamy side. It is not true that a laissez-faire society makes original characters, or that a weak social pressure permits strength of mind to develop. Not only is Anarchic Individualism incompatible with liberty, but it is hopelessly opposed to that Individualism which alone is an ethical good — intellectual independence and moral robustness.

The fact is, that such terms as Individualism or Socialism are not in any way fitted to designate moral ideals, unless they are taken in a sense wholly independent of reference to liberty and legislation.   There is no necessary connection between the moral strength of the Individual and the so-called Individualism of legal and economical machinery ; nor is there any justification for confusing legislative collectivism, under the name of Socialism, with that recognition of the social end which is the basis of *all* possible moral views of Society. I have no doubt that the moral fervour, both of Individualists and of Socialists, arises in great measure from this elementary confusion, by which a doctrinaire theory about legal or economical machinery takes the place of devotion to individual character or to the social purpose. What that purpose is, and how to be fulfilled, *can be learnt only in the concrete* ; and it is our task, without prejudices for abstract titles, to labour at giving a reasonable shape to the innumerable details of the great building of life.

Butler & Tanner, The Selwood Printing Works, Frome, and London.